The Boy who Forgave

The Boy who Forgave

Patrick of Ireland

K.C. Murdarasi

CF4·K

10 9 8 7 6 5 4 3 2 1

Copyright © K.C. Murdarasi 2015

Paperback ISBN: 978-1-78191-677-3

epub ISBN: 978-1-78191-672-8

mobi ISBN: 978-1-78191-673-5

Published by

Christian Focus Publications,

Geanies House, Fearn, Tain, Ross-shire,

IV20 1TW, Scotland, U.K.

Tel: 01862 871011

Fax: 01862 871699

www.christianfocus.com

email: info@christianfocus.com

Cover design by Daniel van Straaten

Cover illustration by Jeff Anderson

American English is used throughout this book

Printed and bound in Denmark by Nørhaven

This book is written in a conversational style. Its use of dialogue is fictional, but used in such a way as to get across facts and history with a relaxed and easily read approach.

Contents

Chapter

Kidnapped!

Kidnapped!

A sharp sea wind blew into Patrick's eyes, making them water so he could hardly see the ship on the western horizon. Far below him, great white waves crashed into rocks that grew smaller and smoother as the coastline edged around into the silted mouth of the river. A little further, down the steeply sloping path he had just climbed, lay Patrick's villa. It was a bit crumbled at the edges; the mosaic floor and the old water pipes needed repairs that no one in Britain had the skills to do anymore, but it was still one of the finest houses in the area. Patrick's father Calpurnius was a *decurion*, a local government official, *and* a deacon, a leader in the church, so his family was pretty important. Calpurnius had gone into the local town that day on official business, taking his wife with him. That meant Patrick was supposed to be in charge of the villa and lands, but there were plenty of servants to take care of everything, so Patrick had decided to climb up the hill and look at the sea, instead. Later, he thought, he might go fishing in the river, or walk the mile or so to the little market village of Bannavem Taburniae, but for now he was content to feel the fresh, cold air on his face and gaze out at a ship that seemed to be on the edge of the world.

It wasn't literally the edge of the world, of course, but it was the edge of the only world that mattered—the Roman Empire. Britain was the furthest corner of the Empire, but it was still Roman. Patrick could speak and write decent Latin, and he knew a fair bit about the history and literature of Rome. True, Britain wasn't as civilized as it once was, or at least so older people said. Patrick was only sixteen, but his elders, with longer memories, said that once, it had been easier and more profitable to trade with the rest of the Empire, when the might of Rome had kept pirate raids away. Once, taxes had been collected like clockwork, and calculated to the last penny. People didn't mind that tax collection was a bit less regular these days. And of course, there must have been a time when there were world-class workmen and builders in Britain, who had made all the houses and technology that the citizens these days couldn't even find anybody to repair. Now, anyone with skill stayed in Italy, and Rome was too busy protecting itself from wandering armies of barbarians to worry about how its citizens in far-flung Britain were getting on.

But still, Britain was Roman. Those islands out there, impossible to see except on the very clearest days, were outside the Empire. The people who lived there were uncivilized, different and dangerous. They spoke a foreign language and knew no Latin. Patrick had never seen any of these wild people, but when he was a child, his father had told him stories of raids from across the sea.

"I remember when I was a younger man, Patrick, before you were born, when the general Maximus tried to become Emperor of Rome," his father would say, as they huddled round the fire on a winter's night. "He nearly succeeded too. He came very close. But in order to make yourself an emperor, you need an army. So Maximus marched out of Britain and took his army with him. It wasn't long before the barbarians came calling, with their battle axes and their wild war cries." Patrick's eyes shone in the firelight as he listened to the familiar tale. "Right up the rivers they came, right into the heart of Britain, with no one to stop them! Here at the coast we tried to protect ourselves, fight them off. Further inland they were taken completely by surprise. Thousands of people taken away as slaves, carried to Ireland!" Patrick gave a little shiver.

"Tell me about the other time, that was even worse!" Calpurnius laughed gently at Patrick's eagerness.

"I was only a child then myself, so I don't remember clearly, but my father, Potitus, told me that it was the worst danger Britain had ever faced! On three sides they came: the Saxons from the east, the Picts from the north, and the Scots from Ireland. They made a pact to steal Britain from out of Rome's hands. Even the soldiers on Hadrian's Wall joined the conspiracy—

9

those who were supposed to protect us! My father said there were piles of dead bodies in every town, every village—such scenes as he could never forget. I remember a little of it myself. I remember it gave me nightmares for years afterwards. But then the Roman army arrived, sent by the Emperor himself, and we were saved. Now, enough of this sombre stuff! Read to me from your Latin book!"

Patrick remembered many evenings like that when he was younger, but these days his father no longer spoke of those times. They didn't seem so entertaining now that most of the Roman army had left Britain and the barbarian raids had started again. It was nothing like those terrible times, of course, Patrick thought, but still it was not impossible that the ship he was watching right now might be full of Irish raiders! He squinted at it, covering his eyes with his hands, and frowned. Actually, it was more than one ship. He could see others behind it, just coming into view. The wind was strong and they were traveling swiftly. They did seem to be coming this way. They could just be trading vessels, of course, but they didn't look quite right to Patrick. He could see them a bit more clearly now and they were a different style to all the Roman ships he'd seen. Maybe they were fishing boats, or they were simply lost. But the ships kept coming straight toward him, not stopping to put down fishing nets.

Patrick started to get nervous. Keeping his eye on the ships, he started back down the hill. He didn't want to look like a coward and go running home just because he had seen a few unfamiliar ships, but what if they really were raiders? He picked up his pace, the wind at his back, and started to jog carefully down the slippery grass. The ships were very close now. They were big. He could see the sails shifting as they started to turn into the mouth of the river. Patrick started to run. He couldn't reach the village before the ships, but surely he could manage to warn the villa. Patrick ran down the hill, and the ships rowed swiftly up the river. By now, he could see the people onboard, and they were not fishermen. He could see weapons lying next to the rowers, ready for use. The ships passed out of sight behind trees and Patrick put on a furious burst of speed to reach the villa. It was only five hundred meters away, four hundred, three hundred—but he could no longer see how close the raiders were, or whether they had landed. He dashed along the path and skidded round the corner into the courtyard.

"*Raiders!*" he wheezed to the female servant who was carrying water to the kitchen. He paused to take a few breaths. "Raiders…" he said again, "…from Ireland. Ships coming down the river now! We need … to protect ourselves!" The servant opened her mouth to say something, but suddenly her hands flew up to her mouth and she dropped the big amphora of water, which smashed into pieces. Patrick didn't understand her reaction until a swift arm snaked round his neck, and held a long knife to his throat.

"Stand still not get hurt," said a man's voice in terrible Latin next to Patrick's ear. The man was breathing heavily; he had obviously sprinted all the way from the riverbank. The servant screamed, and ran into the villa. Over the sound of his own heavy breathing, Patrick could now hear pounding feet. More raiders! He tried to struggle, but the knife pressed more firmly against his neck, cutting him.

"Stand still not get hurt," the voice repeated, and then shouted instructions in a language Patrick couldn't understand. Twenty men flooded into the courtyard and entered the house. Strong hands yanked Patrick's arms behind him and tied them together. Inside the villa Patrick could hear screams. Once again he tried to struggle, but this time he was shoved hard to the ground, jarring his elbow, and his feet were tied loosely together. He rolled over and saw a dark-eyed, heavily scarred face grinning at him.

"Let me go! I'm a Roman citizen! You can't just kidnap me!" The only answer Patrick got was a hard smack on the side of his mouth. The raider stood up and called to his men in the villa, who shouted back. By now, they were returning to the courtyard, dragging servants with them, bound hand and foot like Patrick. The leader pulled Patrick to his feet.

"Go!" he said, pointing to the path that led to the river. He gave the boy a kick to get him started. He was still holding the long knife as if he didn't need much excuse to use it. Reluctantly, Patrick started hobbling down the path, taking tiny steps with his bound legs, and trying not to stumble. Behind him he could hear the servants shouting and crying. There was the sound of a few punches or kicks, and then there was no shouting, only crying.

Down at the river they were marched up a gangplank onto a waiting ship. All the other ships, Patrick assumed, had continued down the river to raid the village. The servants from the villa, and their young master, were shoved into a deep hold at the centre of the ship. With hands and feet tied, there was nothing they could do but sit and watch as the raiders took up their positions at the oars again, and rowed to join the other ships further up the river. Before they even reached Bannavem Taburniae, Patrick could smell smoke. He could see nothing down in the hold, but he could tell from the smell and from the screaming and shouting that much of the village must be on fire. The ship ran aground with a jerk, and the raiders jumped out to join in the attack, leaving just a couple of men with axes to guard the handful of captives. It wasn't long before more people were being thrown into the hold, and more and more. One woman was clutching her sobbing child, who only looked about seven years old.

"What's happening up there?" Patrick asked her.

"They're burning the village," she told him, her eyes wide and frightened. "Raiders came out of nowhere and started grabbing people and setting buildings alight. Some of the men tried to fight back, but it was hopeless. Everyone who fought back was killed, everyone else ..." Her voice tailed off as she looked at the now-crowded hold, into which more and more people were being thrown.

"How many?" asked Patrick.

"In the village? Maybe a thousand people. But I saw the ships going further upriver, too. Maybe they won't go as far as the town, but ..." She trailed off, thinking. Patrick thought, too, about all the other little villages based near the river, so that people could get drinking water and wash their clothes and go fishing. Now the river was bringing them the danger of kidnap, or even worse. The raiders were moving far too quickly for anyone to get a warning to the villages further upstream. There was nothing anyone could do, and there was no one to rescue them. Many of the others in the hold were crying, some quietly and others without holding back. It was only because he was the son of a deacon and a *decurion* that Patrick forced himself not to cry, too.

After an hour or so, Patrick felt the ship start to move. He struggled to stand amidst all the people squeezed into the hold.

"Where are you taking us?" he shouted. Other people also shouted out questions. "You can't do this!" added Patrick. "We're Roman citizens! My father is an important man!" The raiders paid no attention to the people they had kidnapped. They laughed amongst themselves, and then one of them started up a song, and the others joined in. The raiders rowed to the beat of the song, down the river and out to sea, carrying their helpless passengers over the edge of the world.

The rain started somewhere in the middle of the sea, and by the time the ships had arrived at their destination, Patrick and the other captives were soaked through and shivering. He had a fair idea of what was going to happen next. After all, the raiders hadn't rowed all these people across the sea just to kill them. Patrick realized that they were going to sell the captives, along with any valuables they had stolen. Even so, it was a shock to be hauled in front of a crowd of people, along with dozens of other Britons, and see people placing bids for them, just like his father did for cattle. Patrick couldn't see the faces of the bidders, because they had covered their heads against the rain, and he couldn't understand the language, but it was easy to see what was going on. Men held up fingers to show the amount of money, pointed at the slaves they were interested in buying. It was all over before Patrick knew it. One of the men gestured at him, along with a few other young lads, and they were dragged off to the side where some burly men with clubs made sure they didn't try to run away. Patrick could see the man who had bought them handing over some money.

"You can't do this!" he shouted in Latin. "I'm a Roman citizen! I'm the son of a Roman official!" One of the raiders, who was standing nearby, understood what Patrick said, and laughed. He turned to the boy with a mocking smile.

"You see that man over there? He's your new master, boy. It doesn't matter what you were yesterday. You're whatever he says you are now."

Six Years A Slave

The bleating of the sheep was the only sound on the mountain. Patrick shivered and hugged his clothes around him. Above him the sky was low, gray, and steely, while around him on every side stretched empty countryside, wet and hilly, dotted with sheep. The only other things Patrick could see were, in one direction, the wooden structure that was home to him and his fellow slaves, with sheep pens next to it, and in the other direction, on the horizon, the endless sea that lay beyond Ireland.

No amount of begging or threatening helped. Whenever he had managed to explain that he was a Roman citizen, people just laughed at him. That meant nothing over here. Most of the time he couldn't communicate with people, anyway; their language was different from his and they didn't know Latin either. Kicking up a fuss or refusing to go where he was taken just got him beaten. In the end, Patrick had to give in and accept it: he really was a slave. No one from his old life knew where he was, no one in his new life cared about him, and there was nothing he could do to change his situation. He couldn't even run away, because he had no idea where to run to. He was completely helpless.

Patrick felt tears rising to his eyes. He wished he had paid more attention to the Bible when he lived in Britain, or had gone to church more often. His father was a deacon and his grandfather had been a priest, but Patrick had never cared much about religion. He had supposed that the church might be a good career when he was older, maybe, but there was plenty of time for that later. Now, that future had been snatched away from him, and he realized he had spent his youth ignoring the one thing that might be of use to him in this wretched situation—for surely only God could reach him here, at the end of the world! If only he knew how to pray, at least that might help! Alone on the hillside, Patrick felt a powerful urge to try to pray. It was as if God himself *wanted* Patrick to speak to him. Hesitantly at first, Patrick opened his mouth.

"Dear God, dear Father, I'm sorry that I didn't care about you in Britain. I didn't pay attention to your Word in the Bible. I did things I shouldn't have, I know. I don't really know how to pray to you, or worship you, but if you'll forgive me, I'll do my best." Patrick felt as if a weight had lifted off him, a weight he hadn't even been aware of. For the first time since he had been kidnapped he felt a faint smile cross his face. He was still a captive at the far end of the world, but now he knew he was not alone.

Over the weeks and months that followed, Patrick became more and more enthusiastic about praying. He started praying when he got up in the morning, when it was still dark and the cold made his bones ache. He prayed last thing at night when he could hardly keep his eyes open. He prayed when he was out on the hills and forests with the sheep, and when he was in the hut with the other slaves. He prayed in rain, snow, hail, and sunshine, and all the time he felt his love for God increase, and his faith strengthen. All the while, Patrick was also learning the language of Ireland, and finding it easier to communicate with others. He learned that there were other Christians in Ireland, although they were rare. Most people held to the old religion of worshiping fierce gods and goddesses, and believed that the Druids were powerful magicians because of their secret knowledge. Patrick longed for the people of this wild island to know God, who was truly powerful, but he was just one slave in the middle of nowhere; there was not much he could do.

Years passed, and Patrick grew into a man. He did his best to care for the flocks and obey his master, and to share his faith in God with his fellow slaves when he could, but still he dreamed of returning home. He thought about the gentle life he had left behind, across the sea, where there were warm blankets, and nice things to eat, and people to do things for him, instead of the other way around. He thought of his father and mother, and wondered if they were still alive, and if they were thinking about him. Patrick often prayed for his family and his homeland, and told God how much he would he would like to return, and be freed from his slavery. He believed that God could answer his prayers, but even so it took him by surprise when, one night in a dream, he heard the voice of God saying to him, "You will soon set out for your home country."

Patrick awoke the next morning, very excited. He was sure that his dream was a message from God. As far as he could in his situation, he started to make preparations. Patrick sometimes fasted, going without food so that he could concentrate on God, but now instead of refusing the food that was provided, he put it aside so it would be ready for his journey. He also had a little money, given to him by his master on special religious festivals or when Patrick had done something particularly good. He counted up this money, since he knew it could be important for his journey, and knotted it carefully into his clothes.

A few days later, Patrick once again received a message in his dreams: "Look, your ship is ready!" He knew the moment had come. In the dark hut he gathered up the food he had saved, checked he had his money, and carefully stepped over the warm, sleeping forms of the other slaves. He unlatched the door and crept out, past the sheep pens where the restless sheep were gently bleating. It was dark and cold, and Patrick did not know where he was going, but he felt no fear.

Putting the western sea behind him, he started out on his voyage home.

The journey was long and difficult. Patrick was used to the rain and cold by now. He had, after all, spent most of the last six years on the open hills and moors. He was now a lot stronger than the sixteen-year-old boy who had marched here in tears, but he did not know where he was going, and he had to travel the first few days mainly at night in case anyone recognized him and took him back to his master. He soon ran out of food, and it was hard to find a safe and sheltered place to sleep during the day, but gradually he put the miles behind him and no one stopped him.

After a few days, Patrick felt safe enough to travel by day and use a little of his money to buy food, but not too much, because he would need it for the ship. He could not ask directions because he did not know where he was going, but God had told him that his ship was waiting, so Patrick kept on, trying to go roughly east so that he would reach the sea between Ireland and Britain. He knew from his education that Ireland was much smaller than Britain, but it seemed large enough now, as he walked right across it on his own feet. Sometimes Patrick wondered if he had taken the wrong way, but, as always, he prayed day and night, and the sense of peace and assurance he felt about this journey would not leave him.

Eventually, after traveling for weeks, Patrick arrived at a harbor on the western shore, where a ship lay quietly at anchor. It was nightfall by the time he arrived, and he was very tired, so he found a hut near by that was half-full of empty barrels and old ropes, and there he made his bed for the night. Patrick slept longer than he intended, and when he finally made his way along to the harbor the next day, the ship was getting ready to set sail. Excited, Patrick hurried to make enquiries.

"Do you serve on this ship?" he asked a sailor, who was tying elaborate knots in ropes.

"I do."

"When are you setting sail?" Patrick asked. "I have traveled such a long way to find a ship!"

"We sail in less than an hour!" replied the man. "As soon as the last of the cargo is loaded and the final checks are made, we'll be away with the tide."

"That's perfect!" said Patrick. "Can I sail with you? I must get back to Britain, where my family are. I have money to pay for the journey, and if it's not enough I'll happily help to crew the ship."

The sailor shrugged. "I don't see why not. I'll ask the steersman. He's in charge." He finished tying down the barrel he had been securing, and walked off to speak to a scarred, bearded man further along the shore. Patrick's happiness bubbled up inside of him. He had made it away from his captor, he had found the ship God had told him about, and now he was about to go home! His happiness didn't last long, though. The fierce-looking bearded man was stomping up the harbor toward him, looking like thunder.

"You're the lad who wants a lift on my ship, are you?" he said in heavily accented Latin. "Well look: we've got a full crew, we don't take passengers, and we're too busy! So why don't you go and find yourself another ship, and stop bothering my crew when they're trying to work?" He boomed the last words, and turned sharply away. The first sailor that Patrick had spoken to gave him a sympathetic shrug that said, *Sorry, but what can I do?* Patrick nodded his thanks to the man and turned away, his shoulders slumped. He had been so sure that this was the ship God had guided him to! Behind him, the steersman's shouts had attracted the attention of the other sailors, who started asking their colleague what the boss had been yelling about.

Patrick trod slowly back toward the storage hut, since he had nowhere else to go. As he plodded, he started to pray.

"Lord, thank you for bringing me safely this far, and I'm sorry if I'm being impatient. Please continue to guide me in my journey..."

"Hey, you! Hey!" A shout from behind him interrupted Patrick's prayer. It was the sailor he had spoken to. Patrick started to walk back toward the ship.

"Come on, quick, or you'll be too late!" shouted another sailor who was already on the ship. "The boss has changed his mind—come on!" Patrick picked up his feet and ran toward the ship. The sailor he had first spoken to gave him his arm to help him up the steep gangplank, then drew it up after him.

"It seemed a shame to leave a young lad behind, so we talked the boss into it," said the young sailor who had called from the ship. "We told him you seemed like a trustworthy lad. Come on, pledge your faith to us now so we can all be sure of each other."The young man pulled open his tunic, revealing weird tattoos on his chest, and the other sailors nearby did the same. Patrick recognized that they were inviting him to take part in an Irish ceremony of friendship, but he also knew that it involved invoking false gods. Even though he didn't want to offend his new companions, and he certainly didn't want to lose his ride, his conscience wouldn't allow it.

"I'm a Christian," he said, without loosening his own shirt. "We don't invoke the old gods, we worship only one God. Can I instead pledge my friendship by clasping hands or with a kiss?"

"You're a strange lad!" the young sailor said, fastening his tunic up again, but he took the hand that Patrick offered. Patrick clasped hands with each of the sailors in turn, except the scarred steersman, who looked at him darkly, still not keen on taking passengers.

"Cast off!" yelled the steersman suddenly, making Patrick jump. Some of the sailors started to push off from the harbor wall with their oars, while others caught the ropes thrown from the shore, and coiled them tightly. Dark water appeared between the ship and the shore, growing wider and wider as the ship's prow turned toward the sea. Patrick grasped the side of the ship and could hardly keep from laughing with joy. At last, he was going home!

The Longest Way Home

Something was badly wrong. Patrick was no sailor, but even he could see that. The sailors, who only a few hours ago had been good-natured and jokey, now had frowns on their faces, and snapped at Patrick every time they spoke to him. Ropes strained, wood creaked, and waves crashed into the ship in a way that made Patrick very nervous. He did his best to keep out of the sailors' way, and out of the wind and rain that had swept down from the north, but as the hours dragged on and night started to fall, he had to ask what was going on.

"We've been driven off course, that's what's going on!" said the young sailor with the tattoos, struggling with a rope.

"So where are we going to now?" Patrick asked. The young sailor laughed, but he didn't sound as if he found the situation funny.

"Your guess is as good as mine, British boy. This wind will take us wherever it chooses. Maybe right to the bottom of the ocean!"

"Stop distracting my lads!" came a booming voice from the stern of the ship. Patrick peered through the gloom to see the steersman wrestling with the rudder. "If you want to do something useful, pray this storm dies out before the ship breaks up!"

Patrick got the message. He slunk back to the corner where he had been hiding, and prayed for himself and all the men on the ship. It was far too stormy that night to light any lamps, so the night passed in terrifying blackness, full of the sound of the sea's fury, the ship's distress and the men's terror.

The storm continued into the second day. The wind wasn't so strong now, nor the waves so high, but it was still far too strong to try and sail in any other direction, so for a further day the little ship was swept miles off course, with no idea of where they would end up. There was no land in sight, but with the sea being so rough they could have been close to shore without being able to see it. Most of the food had been thrown overboard the day before to make the ship lighter, so there wasn't much left to eat. Patrick saw the steersman glaring at him as he ate his small share —not just a useless body now, but an extra mouth to feed, too.

During the second night, the storm finally died away. The men took it in turns to get some sleep. Sometimes the clouds parted a little and stars could be seen. The sailors who were awake looked intently at them, trying to work out where they must be and charting a course toward land.

When he awoke the next morning, Patrick saw that while most of the sailors were bailing water to keep the ship afloat, some were at the oars, and what was left of the sails were catching the breeze.

"Good morning, sleepyhead!" said the tattooed young sailor. "Why don't you take an oar and we'll get to land sooner?"

"Are we near land?"

"I have no idea how far we are, but I do know it's that way." He gestured toward the rising sun. "Come on, pull your weight!" Patrick did as he was told and soon his back was aching with the effort of pulling the heavy oar. The sailors were tired and hungry but the tension of the last two days had vanished with the storm. They would soon be safe on land.

It was into the afternoon before they sighted land, and early evening before the steersman managed to ease the damaged ship safely to shore.

"We'll sleep on the ship tonight," said the steersman, "and tomorrow we'll try to find a town or a village—if there is one!"

"Doesn't he know where we are?" Patrick asked the kind older sailor he had first met.

"No one knows. We were blown away from the coast and then we sailed back to it, but how far we have traveled in-between, who can say? We'll find some locals tomorrow and they'll tell us where we've landed."

But they didn't find any local people the next day. After they had combed the entire surrounding area, the steersman ordered the crew to pack up anything important and get ready to march. With no food and no way to contact anyone, they could not stay where they were. They walked for days through barren country. There was enough water to drink from little streams and from the rain, but they found no food at all; no cows, no sheep, no pigs, no wild animals—none that they could catch, anyway— and no fruit or vegetables. On and on they walked, until the days turned into weeks. As they became more and more exhausted from hunger, Patrick and the crew were only able to travel shorter and shorter distances each day. The seamen knew how to navigate by day and night, so they could be sure they weren't going in circles, but still they found no trace of civilization.

On the morning of the twenty-eighth day, the steersman marched up to where Patrick was lying and towered over him. With his cheeks and eyes sunken from starvation, the bearded man looked even more terrifying than usual.

"You believe in this Christian God, don't you?" he demanded. "I've heard you saying that he is great and all-powerful. So why don't you pray for us? Don't you realize that we are going to die here? We may never see another human being!" His booming voice had attracted the attention of the rest of the crew, who looked curiously at Patrick from where they sat or lay. Instead of feeling intimidated, Patrick felt an overwhelming sense of confidence that he knew came from God.

"Yes, I do believe in the Lord God, and so should you. Put your faith in God with your whole heart," he said to his companions, "because nothing is impossible for him. He is going to send you so much food today that you will be stuffed, because everything belongs to God and he can meet all of your needs!"

"Today?" asked one of the sailors, "Really?"

"Today," said Patrick. "When you sleep tonight, your stomach will be full."

"If that happens, Briton, I will worship your God too!" said the steersman with a harsh laugh.

Slowly, the crew members picked themselves up and set off on shaky legs, some of them supporting friends who could barely walk. They set off in the same direction they had been traveling for nearly a month. So far, this day was like every other day that they had suffered, but not for long.

"What's that noise? Can you hear it?" one sailor suddenly asked.

"I can hear it too, and I think I can smell something."

"There's something moving over there, look!"

"PIGS!"

Hiccupping with joyful laughter, and trying not to rush and panic the animals, the sailors approached the herd of pigs that had strayed across their path. They drew their swords and knives, and got to work. Soon, the delicious smell of roasting pork filled the valley. Sailors snatched the meat from the fire as soon as it was even barely cooked,

31

swapping it from hand to hand and blowing on it as the hot pork burned their fingers and lips. There was more than enough for everybody. True to his word, the fierce steersman approached Patrick, looking much less fierce than usual.

"You told the truth, Patrick. Your God truly is powerful. Let us all give thanks to the Christian God!" Gladly, the other crew members joined in with prayers of thanks to God for saving them from starvation, and Patrick taught them what he could remember of the hymns he had learned in his youth back in Britain.

The crew stayed in the same place the following day, eating the rest of the pork, to give the weaker crew members a chance to recover their strength. After two nights with full bellies, everyone felt ready to carry on. There still seemed to be no one in this land they had found, despite the pigs, but now there was food every day, as well as wood for fire. The weather also improved so that they weren't shivering in damp clothes every night. They started to come across edible plants, and other things to vary their diet from leftover pork. One day, the young tattooed sailor jogged up to Patrick holding his hand out.

"Look!" he said. "Honey! We found it in the woods." Patrick reached out and took some of the thick golden liquid on his fingers.

"We've dedicated it to Anu, of course, as a sacrifice, since she's the goddess of plenty." Patrick stopped with his fingers halfway to his mouth.

"You sacrificed it to a pagan goddess?" The young sailor nodded. "Then I won't eat it. I believe there is only one true God, and I can't take part in sacrifices to other gods." He wiped the honey back on to the young sailor's hand.

"Sorry, Patrick," said the young sailor. "I didn't realize it would be a problem. In Ireland we try to please all the gods—you never know which one you will need help from."

"There's only God that help comes from," Patrick explained, "and he is the only God you will ever need."

That night, Patrick's sleep was interrupted by a terrible dream. He dreamed that a huge rock fell on him, crushing all the life out of his body. He could not move his arms or legs at all, let alone push the rock off. In his dream he had a sudden feeling that he should call out to the sun.

"Sun! Sun!" he shouted, and immediately in the east the sun rose. The light fell on the terrible weight on top of Patrick and he was freed. Opening his eyes, Patrick saw the light of the real sun coming over the horizon. Patrick was full of relief and gratitude. He realized that the dream had a meaning, and that the sun must represent Jesus Christ, the light of the world. Patrick had not even known how to call out to him in the dream, but Jesus himself had helped Patrick to ask for his help. It was just like when Patrick was in Ireland at first, and God helped him to pray for help. *What amazing grace!* thought Patrick. He knew he could spend his whole life serving God, and he would still never even start to repay such amazing kindness.

A few days later, after over a month of wandering, the crew of the storm-hit ship finally met other human beings. It was the first day since they had found the pigs that they had run out of food, so it was perfect timing. It was so strange to see normal people again, going about their everyday lives! And the villagers were surprised to find a crew of shipwrecked sailors so far from the coast. Soon, after getting directions and supplies, it was time for the group to split up. The steersman set out for a large coastal town to try and raise capital for a new ship. Some of the crew followed him, while others set off to try their fortune on other ships, or even in other professions. A few decided to stay in the area they had ended up in, at least for the time being.

After speaking to the villagers, and getting as good an idea of the geography as they could give him, Patrick headed off by himself in the direction that seemed most likely to lead back to his family. It was strange to be on his own again, a free man. Only a month earlier he had thought he was going straight home, but the ship that God had led him to had taken a very different path. The hardships he and the crew members had suffered had shown the sailors, and Patrick, just how powerful God was, and how near. Patrick might be going back to his family home now, but he realized that his real home was in God, and God was with him wherever he went.

Patrick traveled slowly, getting directions from the people he met, sometimes taking wrong turns and having to retrace days of walking. He took on different kinds of work for a day or so to earn his keep, and wherever he found churches or Christian communities he never missed the chance to hear a sermon or reading from the Bible, or attend a prayer meeting. He drank up the religion that he had neglected as a child. There was so much to learn! Patrick realized that he had been starving for God's Word in Ireland as much as he had been starving for food after the shipwreck. He decided that he would never neglect the Word of God again. From now on, he would live his life for Jesus Christ.

Trudging along the weary road home, looking for the next farm to offer him work or shelter on the way, Patrick thought about the amazing story he would have to tell his family and friends. Enough adventure for a lifetime!

Called by God

It took Calpurnius a moment to recognize the man standing in front of him.

"Patrick? Patrick, is that you?"

"Yes, Father, it's me!" Patrick laughed, as his father pulled him into a bear hug. "I have finally returned."

"I thought you were dead!" said Calpurnius, barely holding back tears. Turning to the servant who was hovering, wondering what was going on, Calpurnius ordered, "Go and fetch your mistress!" He turned back to Patrick. "Your mother will be so happy to see you! You must tell me where you have been all these years! How did you escape from the raiders? Where did they take you?" He asked so many questions that Patrick did not even have a chance to start answering him. With his arm around his son, Calpurnius led Patrick along a dark corridor to a living room where a small fire was burning. It was all new to Patrick. The house he had grown up in was gone. He had taken the old path up from the village, but only burned-out ruins were left. The orchard had gone wild and most of the fields were grown over with grass. Long years had passed since that day when the raiders had taken Patrick and torched his house, and it looked like no one had touched the old villa since then.

"Patrick!" A woman's voice pulled Patrick back to the present. He turned to see his mother rushing toward him. It was wonderful to see his mother again, after he had thought so often that he never would, but he was shaken by how much she had aged. She was younger than Calpurnius, but now she almost looked older. Life must have been hard for her in the intervening years—and losing her only son to pirates would not have helped.

"Oh, Patrick," his mother sobbed, not even trying to restrain her sobs, "they told me in the village that a young man had been asking where we lived, but I never dreamed, I never dared hope it could be you! I can't believe you're alive! Thank God!" It was a long time before Patrick's mother stopped crying, and even longer before he was able to tell them what had happened to him, and where he had been all these years. He had not even finished his story before his mother jumped up and called the servants.

"We must have a banquet! We must invite all of our relatives, all our friends—and the leaders of the church, since you are such a man of God now. I will go and give orders to the servants!"

Patrick sat back as his mother started organizing. Calpurnius caught his eye and they shared a little smile at the whirlwind of activity they were both so accustomed to. It was just like old times.

"Oh, Patrick," said his mother, holding her son's face in her hands when she had finally finished her organizing, "promise me you will never go away again!"

Patrick laughed a little uncomfortably.

"I can't promise you that, Mother! I don't know where the rest of my life will take me. But I can't see any reason for leaving again soon!" Seeing that her face still looked anxious, Patrick added, "Don't worry, Mother. Bannavem Taburniae will always be my home. I have come back home."

The banquet was the grandest meal Patrick had had in years, the grandest he could remember, but still, it seemed to him that life in his old village was smaller, somehow. The new house was smaller, of course. The little dining room made the large number of people seem even larger, and noisier, as they greeted each other, congratulated Patrick on his return, and asked him dozens of questions. The new house was much easier to defend, with high walls and smaller windows, and gates sealing off the courtyard from the outside world. It was also inside the village, not isolated, so that everyone could band together to defend themselves if another attack came.

It wasn't just the house, though. The people, too, seemed to have shrunk into themselves more. The clothes the guests were wearing had been repaired often, and more people wore simple, local-made clothes than before—sheepskin, wool and coarse linen. There was less discussion of affairs in Gaul or Italy around the table. It was hard for Patrick to decide whether it was his homeland that had changed, or whether he had just remembered it wrongly during his time as a slave. Either way, it seemed to him as if Britain was starting to become as cut off from the Empire as Ireland was! Fortunately, the people of Bannavem Taburniae had not turned away from the true faith, and it was wonderful for Patrick to be able to talk about God with the deacons and priests who were friends of his father.

The food was good, the company was warm, the conversation was animated, and the feast went on well into the night. Patrick was exhausted by the time he finally climbed into his bed. His head was whirling, and he expected his dreams to be full of the evening's fun, but he could never have predicted what he would dream about, instead.

A man was approaching him. In the mysterious way of dreams, Patrick somehow knew that the man's name was Victoricus, even though he was a stranger. Victoricus was carrying letters—hundreds of letters, perhaps thousands! There were too many to count, but although they were far too many for a man to carry, in the dream Victoricus did not drop a single one. He walked up to Patrick, picked out one of the letters, and held it out to him. Patrick took it and opened it. At the top was written "The Voice of the Irish". Patrick started reading the letter, but all of a sudden he could hear dozens of voices calling in unison: "Holy man, we beg you to come and walk among us again!" Patrick recognized the voices. They were the people who lived in the forest of Foclut, near the western sea—the area where Patrick had been a slave! The desperation in their voices was heartbreaking. Patrick tried to read the letter, but his eyes filled with tears and he couldn't go on. He shut his eyes, and when he opened them again they were still filled with tears, but now he was in the little bedroom in his parents' new house, and he was awake.

Patrick lay still until he had regained control of his emotions, but he could not shake the impression that the dream was a message for him. God was speaking to him on behalf of the Irish, asking him to go back. Never once had Patrick considered deliberately returning to the land that had stolen him. Now, it looked as if he would have to.

Patrick spent several days praying about the vision, talking to God and testing whether this really was the plan for his life. It didn't seem to make any sense. Yes, he had been to Ireland, so he knew the territory and the language, but he had been there as a slave. Who would listen to a runaway slave? And then there was his education—or lack of it. Patrick knew that his Latin was fairly simple, rusty from years of hardly hearing it, and he spoke no Greek at all. It made it harder for him to study the important books of theology that a missionary should understand. Plus, Patrick felt inadequate when it came to prayer. Yes, he prayed all the time, and had done since he was a teenager, but no one had ever taught him how to pray. His prayers were simple, cries of fear or loneliness, or expressions of joy and gratitude. He didn't know how to pray like a missionary should!

On the last point, at least, the Lord offered him some assurance. Once again, Patrick had a vivid dream. He could hear someone speaking close to him—so close that Patrick could not tell whether the voice was coming from beside him, or inside him! The voice spoke in a language that Patrick could not understand, but he could tell it was a prayer. The prayer came to an end, and suddenly Patrick could understand the final words: "He who gave his life for you, he is the one who speaks within you." Patrick was so happy to think that Jesus himself was speaking to God the Father on his behalf, just as it said in the Bible!

One more time, in his sleep, he had a vision of someone praying inside him. This time the voice spoke not in words, but in sighs and groans. Patrick was confused, but at the end of the prayer it suddenly became clear that the voice was from the Holy Spirit. He was helping Patrick to pray! Again, it was just like the promise in the Bible that when we don't know what to pray, the Spirit helps us with "sighs too deep for utterance." With Jesus and the Holy Spirit helping him to pray, Patrick could no longer use his poor prayer skills as an excuse!

By now, Patrick was certain that his path definitely was taking him back to Ireland. That meant he had to tackle the difficult subject with his father and mother. They were only just getting used to the idea that Patrick was back to stay, so it was very difficult news to hear that he was planning to go back to the very place where he had been held as a slave.

"I'm not going back straightaway, Mother," Patrick said, trying to comfort her. Tears rolled down her cheeks as she looked at her son. "It probably won't be for a long time. I have to get some theological training first, and I think I should spend some time serving in the church."

"Years?" asked his mother, hopefully.

"Yes, perhaps years," said Patrick. "I've been praying about it, and even though I'm sure I'm supposed to go back to Ireland some day, I don't get the sense that it's going to happen soon."

"Oh, thank the Lord!" said his mother, finally starting to cheer up. Patrick's father, too, looked relieved.

"There's no sense in rushing something like this," he said. It was sensible advice, but Patrick thought he could see in his father's face the hope that, if they just waited, Patrick would forget all about this rash idea.

"I will need to start preparing, though," Patrick said, determined to show them that this wasn't a whim he was going to forget about. "I will travel south to the wonderful centres of Christian study that

I have heard about. I believe that I will find educated and experienced teachers there who will help me to understand the Bible better, and explain all the mysterious things that I ought to understand." At his words about going away to study, Patrick's mother started crying again, as if he was talking about leaving that afternoon. Patrick decided it was best to drop the subject, at least for the time being.

Even though he knew he would eventually have to leave, Patrick decided that he should get more involved with the local church. It might not offer the kind of education that he would eventually need, but it would help him to grow spiritually and get to know God better. Patrick enjoyed serving the local congregation in Bannavem Taburniae, and seeing church life in the nearby bigger town. He helped to run his parents' estate, which gave him useful experience of directing people and planning. Months passed and years passed, and Patrick knew that his parents hoped he had forgotten all about his idea of going back to Ireland, but he could never forget. Eventually, the time seemed right to travel in search of training in theology and mission. There were many issues he felt he needed to understand better.

Patrick had heard of the British monk Pelagius, who said that human beings could be good through their own efforts, and did not need help from God. Pelagius had been in Rome while Patrick was a slave in Ireland, and although the church did not accept his ideas, they had become popular with a lot of people. Those who agreed with Pelagius said that Jesus had come to Earth and died, not to save people from their sins, but just as a sort of good example to follow. Patrick was sure that wasn't right. He knew himself that he needed God's help to do the right thing and avoid temptation. But he didn't have the education or the experience to give a convincing counter-argument. He knew that Arian ideas were also popular in some parts of the Empire— people who claimed that Jesus was really not God at all, but had been created by God. Again, Patrick felt that he needed more experience of studying what the Bible said about this, and learning from wise Christians. Only then would he be ready to take the message of the true God to the people of Ireland.

It was hard for Patrick to say goodbye to his parents after he had got to know them again.

"Please don't cry, Mother," he said. "At least this time we can say goodbye! And I am not being taken as a slave. I am free to return to you whenever I like!" Calpurnius put his arm around his wife.

"We will both miss you, Patrick, but you are a grown man and you must do what you believe is right. Go south, become a great scholar and make us proud!"

Patrick doubted he would ever make a great scholar, but he appreciated his parents' faith in him.

"Thank you, Father. Goodbye, God bless you, and I promise I will return!"

To Go or Not to Go

It was a very different Patrick who returned to his home years later, and a very different Calpurnius who greeted him.

"Patrick! My boy! It is wonderful to see you again," said the old deacon. Patrick smiled and hugged his father, but he couldn't help thinking that the greeting wasn't exactly accurate. Patrick was not a boy now, not by any stretch of the imagination. Instead, he was a mature man with the first streaks of grey in his hair, and the kinds of aches and pains from the road that indicated that middle age was not far away. Calpurnius, on the other hand, was well past middle age. His hair was entirely grey, the lines in his face had deepened and his back was a little stooped. He had become an old man.

"Come in, come in!" Calpurnius encouraged Patrick, "And introduce me to your companions."

"These are friends of mine from the community where I studied," said Patrick, presenting them to his father.

"We came to hear the bishop Germanus debate with the followers of Pelagius, and when Patrick invited us to visit his home while we were here, we were delighted!" said the eldest.

"And we are delighted to have you!" replied Calpurnius. "You honor our humble home."

Patrick enjoyed being back with his parents, even though it hardly felt like home after all the time he had spent far away. Bannavem Taburniae seemed smaller and quieter than he remembered, and his life in the ruined villa up on the hill felt like a story from another time. This was where he had been born, of course, but he had been born again, as a Christian, over in Ireland, and he had grown so much in the community where he had spent the last few years that he hardly felt like he had a true home to come back to. The fact that he would one day go back to Ireland also made it impossible for him to truly settle down anywhere. Patrick was resigned to the fact that in this life he was a pilgrim and wanderer, but the wise Augustine, some of whose writings Patrick had read, said that our true home is in the eternal city of God—heaven. That, and the fact that God was with him wherever he went, comforted Patrick more than having a real home to go to.

The visit with his friends was lovely, and Patrick enjoyed showing them around and introducing them to the people he remembered, but all too soon they had to leave. Alone in Bannavem Taburniae with his parents again, Patrick knew that he would have to bring up the subject they did not want to talk about—his return to Ireland.

It was particularly difficult because throughout the time that his friends had been there, his mother and father had said things—just little things—that suggested that they hoped he had given up on that silly idea. His mother talked about finding him a wife, and his father mentioned the long-term plans for the estate, as if Patrick was going to be around forever. His companions knew about his plans to return to Ireland—he had told them as soon as he had joined their community—and they sometimes gave him confused looks when his parents said these things. Patrick had just shrugged at the time, and tried to explain later that his parents didn't want him to go. His companions promised to pray for him as he tried to persuade them that it was the right thing to do.

Now the time had come to start that persuasion. Patrick decided to tackle the subject soon after his friends had gone back south to rejoin Germanus. Gathered around the fire with his wife and son, Calpurnius had once again referred to the future of the estate as if Patrick would be there to oversee it, and this time Patrick knew he couldn't let it go. He had not forgotten about Ireland. It was time to say the words he knew his parents were hoping not to hear.

"Father, Mother, I don't want you to think that I'm not enjoying being back with you, because I am. I have missed you during these last years, and I would love to spend the rest of my life here with you, to help you in your old age and look after the estate, and perhaps get married. But I truly believe that the Lord has called me to go to Ireland. It was a long time ago that I had that dream, the one I told you about, but the feeling hasn't gone away. I can't settle down here, no matter how much I want to; the road ahead of me leads to Ireland."

Calpurnius' face fell in disappointment, and it made him look even older. Beside him, his wife gently dabbed her eyes. Patrick wished he didn't have to leave his parents now that they were approaching their final years on earth, but he was only telling the truth—God had told him to go to Ireland.

"These last few years I have been preparing for the work that I know lies ahead," Patrick continued. "I have been getting to know the Bible and other Christian writings. I've been finding out more about prayer, worship, and self-discipline. I feel that I am ready now, ready to take the good news about Jesus to the people of Ireland."

"But Patrick!" interjected his mother, "Those people kidnapped you! They held you as a slave!"

"It probably won't be exactly the same people who kidnapped me, Mother. And even if it is, God's forgiveness extends to everyone. He even forgave the people who killed him while they were crucifying him!"

"Your mother has a point, though," Calpurnius said slowly. "Are you sure this is the right thing for you?

What if something happens to you? You may just end up being enslaved again. You might spend more years wasting your life on a damp Irish mountainside, unable to tell anyone about anything."

"That might happen, it's true," Patrick replied, placing his hand on his mother's shoulder to comfort her from the thought, "but it is God who has told me to go to Ireland, and he knows why he is sending me. Even if I just end up being kidnapped again, God already knew that would happen, and has still called me to go. He has a plan for me, and his plans are perfect —however strange they may seem at the time. That's what my years as a slave taught me."

Calpurnius ran a hand through his thick grey hair, shaking his head sadly.

"Your mind is obviously made up, Patrick. I see that we can't persuade you otherwise—although I don't think your mother is going to give up trying!" he added, with a wry smile for his wife. "If you are being called as a missionary to Ireland then we will have to contact the church authorities and ask them to send you to Ireland as a missionary. You had better go and meet with the local bishop."

Patrick felt a sense of relief that he had straightened things out with his parents, even if they weren't happy about the idea of their son disappearing away to Ireland again. He had thought that breaking his news to his parents would be the hard part. He wasn't prepared for opposition from the church, too.

Patrick was full of enthusiasm on the day he went to be presented to the bishop and elders of the church in the nearby city. He knew that he was finally setting out on the road that God had revealed to him all those years ago. Perhaps quite soon he would be on a ship, bound for Ireland, with the backing of the local church! The thought knotted his stomach with nervousness, but it was the cause that he had decided to devote his life to, so it was also exciting that he was getting so close! Patrick had met the bishop and the elders before, of course, but not in such a formal situation. Calpurnius, as a deacon, presented Patrick to the group of seated older men, and stated the purpose of the meeting.

"Thank you for agreeing to meet us today," he said. "As you know, my son Patrick has been called by God to serve the people of Ireland. He wants to ask for your blessing, support, and guidance." Calpurnius gestured toward Patrick, who was standing slightly behind him, somewhat nervously. "You can see for yourselves that he is a grown man now. He can answer any questions you want to put to him." Leaving the floor to Patrick, Calpurnius sat down with the other church leaders.

The bishop, a kindly-looking man but with a smile that always seemed a little bored, gestured for Patrick to come further forward.

"Good morning, Patrick. Thank you for coming to see us. We have heard about your enthusiasm for Ireland from your father, of course, but we want to hear it in your own words. Why do you feel God might have called you to Ireland?"

Patrick was surprised by the doubt in the bishop's voice, but he supposed that church elders had to make sure that people were really following God's leading, and not just their own imaginations. Starting with his kidnap when he was sixteen, and working all the way up to the vivid dream about Victoricus and the letter from the Irish, Patrick told the elders the story of his life.

"And so I traveled south and spent time with a religious community, learning more about God and the Bible and the Christian life. Now I have returned, after many years, and it seems like the right time to obey what God commanded, and go to Ireland."

The bishop smiled and nodded gently. Patrick looked around the faces of the elders. Some were also smiling encouragingly, others looked more serious.

"Thank you for sharing that with us, Patrick. It was wonderful to hear the story of how God has worked in your life over the years since you were stolen from your home. It is truly a miracle to see you restored to your family! As for the other matter, of your going to Ireland — naturally, the elders and I will have to spend some time in prayer and consultation."

"Oh yes, of course," said Patrick, feeling a little foolish. He had imagined that they would give him their blessing there and then, but of course they would have to give it some thought. He couldn't help feeling a bit disappointed; he had wound himself up to hear their decision, and now he would have to go home without one.

"Come back next month, Patrick, and see us again. I am sure that by then we will have a decision for you."

"Of course, thank you," said Calpurnius, rising from his chair and ushering Patrick out of the room. "Thank you for seeing us."

The next month passed easily enough. Patrick had old friends to catch up with and family members to visit, and there was always something to be organized or recorded for the administration of the estate. As the weeks passed, however, he often found himself thinking about the bishop and the elders, and what their decision would be. Surely they would agree to send him to Ireland with the backing of the church? Once again, Patrick was nervous and excited when he and Calpurnius traveled into the town to hear the verdict.

The bishop welcomed Patrick with his kind but bored smile.

"Ah, Patrick! Good of you to come back so punctually." He spoke in Latin. Last time he had spoken the British language, which Patrick was more comfortable with, but he returned the greeting in Latin.

"Thank you for meeting me. I'm very keen to hear your decision about my call to Ireland."

"Yes, your call to Ireland," said the bishop. "Well, Patrick, we have given the matter a lot of thought. We have considered the practicalities, which perhaps may not have occurred to you. For instance, to go alone to Ireland, or to lead a small team, you would need to be a bishop. Otherwise, how would you be able to make priests in Ireland, if you managed to establish a church? It's a very serious step to make someone a bishop, and it's an act that requires three other bishops to carry it out! I would have to get the agreement of my colleagues in other cities, so that you could truly be a representative of the British church."

Patrick nodded. It did sound very serious, but so was giving your life to serve God in a foreign country. He would happily become a bishop to do that.

"Secondly," the bishop went on, "there's the question of money. It is quite an undertaking. You mentioned that some of your colleagues from the community have said they would be willing to go to Ireland with you. Assuming they stick to that decision, the local church would have to support quite a number of men. It's not just the question of raising funds, but also of getting them to you on that barbarous island."

"As for that," said Calpurnius, "Patrick will, of course, have his share of the estate. He can convert it into cash to help him in his work in Ireland." The bishop smiled again, as if he had heard all of this before.

"That is extremely generous of you, Calpurnius, but even the profits from the sale of your whole estate are unlikely to last Patrick for his whole life, if he is blessed with long life." He didn't say that a long life wasn't very likely for a Briton in Ireland, but he didn't need to; Patrick could read it in his face.

"Finally, there is the question of your educational status. I can see that you understand Latin, and you've clearly had an…adequate…education. But you are not highly educated, are you? Do you really feel that you are competent for leading a team of workers in Ireland, and for setting up churches and training new Christians to become priests?"

Patrick had started to blush as all of his shortcomings were laid out before him, but he knew he had to say something.

"I know I am not highly educated, but I do know the Bible, and I have studied the Christian life. I am not an expert in theology, but I understand God's truth. And even if I am not the sort of person you would normally choose for a mission like this, I am the person that God chose. Doesn't the Bible say that God chose the weak things of the world to shame the wise and powerful? I may be a 'weak thing', but God can use me."

The bishop nodded. "That may well be true, Patrick. And it is not our decision to prevent you from going to Ireland. But we have decided that you should wait. You need to be sure of your calling, and we need to be sure that you are mature enough to be a bishop. Come back to us in a year or two." Patrick's face fell. He looked along the row of elders, but there was only one encouraging face—Proditus, with whom he was friends. All the others looked either sceptical or stern. Looking at them, Patrick couldn't even summon the spirit to argue.

"Thank you for meeting me," he said in a quiet voice, and left.

The following months were very hard for Patrick. He found it difficult to come to terms with the decision of the local church. Doubts started to creep into his mind. He knew that it wasn't just the elders who doubted him. When he was down in the village once, coming out of a shop, he heard someone outside mention his name. He paused, still in the dark doorway where they couldn't see him, and heard a villager, someone he didn't know, speaking about him.

"I mean, Ireland! Of all the places in the world to throw yourself away!"

"You'd think he'd know better. He must know what they're like. Isn't it true that he was kidnapped by the Irish himself?"

"Yes, he was! I remember that day. My family were lucky to get away without being taken ourselves. And he thinks it's a wonderful idea to go back over there, to those thieves and murderers and who knows what else! I tell you what, it would take more than a message from God to make me go over there! They don't *deserve* God, those people!"

"You're right. It's ridiculous to throw away your life for a bunch of bloodthirsty heathens. I wouldn't spit on them if they were on fire! I hope the stupid man sees sense."

The villagers walked on, and left Patrick feeling dejected. Was he really stupid? Was he wasting his life? Could it be that he was wrong about what God wanted him to do? Month followed month, and Patrick's thoughts became bleaker and bleaker. He was just about ready to give up, when one day, in town, he ran into his friend, Proditus, the elder.

"Patrick! It's good to see you. How are you, and how are your family?" The two men chatted for a while about everyday things, until Proditus said, "When are you coming back to see the bishop and the elders? It has been a long time now. Shouldn't you set up another meeting?"

Patrick looked downcast. "Do you think there's any point? Won't they just say the same things again? I don't think they'll even consider me a suitable candidate!"

"Well I do, for one!" said Proditus. "In fact, I think you *ought* to be a bishop, and I'm prepared to speak up for you."

"Thank you!" said Patrick, and he did his best to look enthusiastic, but in fact he felt anything but. This long period of waiting had made him wonder if he was cut out to be a missionary after all. He knew he would have to spend some serious time in prayer before he decided to meet the elders again.

Patrick was always devoted to prayer, but over the next few days he spent more time and energy on it than ever before. He poured out his feelings before God, telling him how he felt embarrassed by the church's low opinion of him, and afraid of being rejected again. His pride was hurt and his confidence was knocked. Perhaps he wasn't the right person, and God should send someone else? As he prayed, slowly Patrick began to feel more peaceful. His eyes were opened to see the situation from God's point of view, not just his own. The point wasn't whether Patrick wanted to go to Ireland, or whether the church wanted to send him, or whether he felt qualified to go. The point was that the people of Ireland needed him, and God had chosen to send Patrick in order to meet that need. At the end of all his praying, Patrick felt more humble than he had before, but also more certain.

Perhaps Patrick's new attitude impressed the local bishop and the elders, or perhaps it was Proditus' confidence in Patrick. Either way, by the end of the third meeting, the bishop had agreed to gather his colleagues from other parts of Britain to make Patrick a bishop – the Bishop to the Irish!

Back to Ireland

"Careful with that bag! Pass it over here!" sailors shouted to each other as they made their boat ready and stowed the luggage. Patrick watched them moving his belongings and thought about the last time he had made this trip, when he was a sixteen-year-old boy. That time he had been dragged away with nothing but the clothes he was wearing. Now, he was taking clothes and money, books and writing materials, and all the equipment he would need to start a new life as a missionary. However, this time he would not be one helpless boy among thousands of captives, but the leader of a small group of missionaries who had volunteered to go.

"Is it strange, Patrick, seeing everything packed up in a little boat, as if a whole life could be tied into bags and stowed away?" Patrick turned to see Secundinus smiling kindly at him.

"It is a little strange to think that those things may be my only contact with Britain for the rest of my life. But I was actually thinking about how glad I am that I have a group of companions and helpers who are willing to come with me."

"We believe in your call, Patrick," said Lomman, who had heard their conversation. "We have, ever since you joined our community to learn more about God, and told us the reason why. It will be a privilege to see what God will do through you, now that your vision is finally coming true!"

"Thank you, my friends!" said Patrick warmly. "Come on, let's join together in prayer. It looks as if we will be ready to sail shortly, and I have had bad experiences at sea before!" They called the other travelers over, and bowed their heads together as they asked God to watch over their journey, and to give them the strength and courage they would need for their exciting but terrifying mission.

A sailor called to let them know their boat was ready to sail, and they all made their way up the gangplank. Patrick looked down at the dust on his feet—British dust. When the wind and the rain washed it away, his last contact with British soil would be gone. Patrick felt the ship move away from the shore, heard the slap of ropes being thrown and wound up. He thought of his parents, far away in BannavemTaburniae, and of the pain of parting from them once again. He thought of his home church and his friends. Then he walked to the other side of the ship and turned his face across the dark sea, toward Ireland. He knew that was where his future lay, and he was ready to step into it bravely.

Patrick needed all his bravery sooner than he had hoped. They had been on land for less than an hour, in the spot they had chosen to start their mission, when an angry-looking man rushed toward them, surrounded by a group of strong men, carrying weapons.

"Who are you? What do you want here?" he demanded. "My servant says you've come to steal the pigs!"

But the fact that Patrick and his friends were carrying no weapons and the pigs were still where the servant had left them gave Patrick a chance to try and establish a friendlier relationship. Better that than a brawl for his first encounter back in Ireland.

"I am Patrick, from Britain," he explained. "These are my companions. We are followers of Jesus Christ and have come to Ireland to teach the people about the God we worship. We have not touched your pigs; please count them if you don't believe us. We are not here to steal or to cause any harm. In fact, the one we follow teaches us that we should treat others the way we would wish to be treated ourselves, and even love our enemies."

The master, who had been listening carefully to Patrick's speech, waved to his men to put their weapons away. He shook his head in bewilderment.

"I consider myself a good judge of character," he said. "Looking at your face, I can see that you're telling the truth. But even so, I don't understand what I'm hearing. You have come across the sea just to tell people about your god? Why? What is so special about him?"

"The God we serve is the only true God, who made the heavens and the earth," said Patrick. "But more than that, he sent his Son to live amongst human beings and even to die in our place. I would be glad to tell you all about him."

"And I would be happy to hear about it!" said the man, smiling for the first time in the conversation, and holding his hands out to Patrick and his friends. "My name is Dichu, and I own all of the land around here. Come with me to my home. You shall stay with me tonight, and tell me all about this God who died."

Dichu was just as open to learning about Jesus as he had claimed. He took the group back to his house, which was actually a fair-sized fortress on a hill, and treated them as welcome guests for several days. Patrick spent the time teaching Dichu about Jesus Christ and the Bible, and explaining that the 'gods' of the pagan religion were just evil demons that were powerless in comparison to the God who had made everything that existed. Dichu listened carefully to what Patrick said and asked lots of questions until his mind was made up.

"I believe you are an honest and good man, Patrick, and I believe what you tell me about Jesus dying to save human beings. I had heard of Jesus before, but no one had ever explained to me about God's plan to save us from our sins. I want to follow Jesus. Please make preparations for the mysterious rite called 'baptism'!"

Patrick and his companions were thrilled to have made their first convert to Christianity practically as soon as they had set foot on the Irish mainland, but it was even better than that. Dichu had been telling the truth about owning all the land round about. He was a rich and important man who would speak up for the Christian faith to other important Irish chiefs. It gave the 'foreign' religion some useful credibility. But perhaps best of all, Dichu gave Patrick his first church in Ireland!

"It's just a barn, really," he told them, "but you can do whatever you need to with it. I'm giving you the hill it stands on, too."

"God bless you for your generosity, Dichu," said Patrick.

"God has already blessed me by sending me messengers to show me the truth!" replied Dichu, smiling. "Now go and set up your church!"

Even though Dichu was a generous host, Patrick knew that he had to travel further into Ireland, to reach people who had never heard of the true God. Taking only what they could carry, and leaving their heavier possessions with Dichu, Patrick and his companions began their missionary journeys within Ireland.

"Which city will we visit first, Patrick?" asked Lomman. "Are we going to start with the largest?"

"There aren't any big cities in Ireland," corrected Patrick. "The people here live in tribes, arranged around the fortresses of their chiefs and kings. There are villages and towns, but no cities like the ones we are used to, with civil government and public buildings"

"How will we spread the good news about Jesus, then?" asked Lomman. "How will we reach people if there are no cities that citizens visit to carry out business or politics, or to pay their rents and taxes? Are we going to visit every village and farm in Ireland?"

"No," said Patrick, "we will approach the chiefs and kings first. They are the equivalent of the cities in the Empire. They are the ones who offer safety and demand loyalty. They are the ones that oversee business and dictate the politics, and they are the ones that rents and taxes are paid to. Dichu has told me all about the local chiefs and kings and high kings in this area. That is where we will start."

And so Patrick's missionary journeys around Ireland began. Although they often returned to Dichu's territory, and their first church, gradually they made contact with chiefs and kings, and their subjects, further and further out. Very few were as quick to accept Christianity as Dichu had been, and Patrick knew he had to tread carefully. Roman citizenship would be no protection to him or his companions on this wild island beyond the Empire.

One method that Patrick found useful was to offer payment to a local chief for protection while he passed through his lands. It gave Patrick a connection to the chief, even if it was only a financial transaction, but often the chief would provide men to accompany the little group as they moved about his territory. Seeing the Christians with the chief's protectors reassured the local people that they were not enemies to be feared, and that made them more willing to listen to Patrick's message. At the same time, Patrick knew that paying money to the chiefs made them more likely to accept his message too; status was very important in Ireland, and everyone knew who was higher or lower on the ladder. People with no land and no property were looked down upon. So far, Patrick only had a tiny piece of land, courtesy of Dichu, but it made a difference, and being able to pay his way made an impression, too. The Irish chiefs and kings were proud men. They would not be prepared to lower themselves to accept a religion spread by beggars. Patrick often thanked God for his family inheritance and the generosity of supporters in Britain that made his 'security payments' possible.

Gradually, the number of Christians in the area began to grow. Patrick's barn-church started to fill up, not only with Dichu and his family, but also with more and more of his servants and tenants, and even people from beyond Dichu's property. Journey after journey, Patrick and his helpers made more and more disciples, and set up new churches. As months passed, and then years, some of the new Christians became mature and knowledgeable enough to lead churches themselves, while others joined Patrick on his travels. Patrick and the men who had come with him from Britain no longer had to go everywhere together for safety and support; now they had a large group of helpers, and were able to split up and lead little missions individually. One of these little missions yielded a major breakthrough.

At a settlement on the River Boyne called 'The Ford of the Alder', an Irish prince called Fedilmid lived with his wife and son. Lomman, Patrick's companion, set out up the river Boyne to visit this settlement and teach the story of Jesus to whoever was prepared to listen. To Lomman's delight, he was received warmly.

"Surely that's a British accent?" asked the princess excitedly when she was introduced to Lomman.

"Yes it is, my lady," confirmed Lomman. "I came from Britain with Patrick, the bishop, to spread the news about Jesus Christ to Ireland."

"How wonderful!" said the princess, switching into the British language. "I come from Britain! My father was a local ruler there. It's so good to meet a fellow Briton! Please, accept the hospitality of my house!"

Lomman was happy to comply, and more than happy when first the princess's son, Fortchernn, and soon afterward the princess herself, accepted the good news about Jesus and became Christians. After that, it wasn't long before her husband, Fedilmid, also embraced his family's new faith.

"You can return to your master, Patrick, and tell him that I have granted him this land to build a church," Fedilmid told Lomman after he and his family had been baptized as Christians. "Tell him to send someone to be our priest. You and your companions will always be sure of our hospitality and our protection."

Lomman thanked Fedilmid warmly for his generosity, and prayed for the family before saying goodbye. As he sailed back down the Boyne to rejoin Patrick, Lomman's heart swelled with excitement and with gratitude to God. He knew that Patrick would be thrilled, too. It wasn't just the family of new Christians, or the grant of land to build a new church, there was something much more significant than that: Fedilmid was no ordinary prince—he was the son of Laoghaire, High King of the whole region!

Fighting against the Darkness

Fire glowed through the night from the hilltop. Not far away, standing in darkness, two men wearing long robes and holding long staffs looked angrily at the flames that rose into the night.

"It is that Christian, Patrick," said one. "He has dared to enter the kingdom of our High King Laoghaire."

"This is a fire," said the other, meaningfully, "that must be put out swiftly, or else it will burn forever here." The first druid nodded his agreement. The fire they were talking about was not the one keeping Patrick and his companions warm but the fire of Patrick's teaching, which was spreading to more and more people, threatening to burn away the old traditions that the two men stood for. As druids, they were the keepers of the old knowledge, passed down by word of mouth and memorized—too sacred ever to be written down. They guarded the history of the kings and chiefs, but also the knowledge about the traditional gods of Ireland, and what worship they demanded from their followers, everything from prayers and incantations to extreme measures like human sacrifice. And they were the keepers of magic and sorcery, casting spells to terrify common people and win the favor of kings. Now this group of missionaries and their many converts, were threatening all of that.

"Laoghaire will never accept this foreign religion. He will not tolerate it within his lands," said the first druid. The second druid said nothing. This fire was the greatest threat that had ever faced the worship of the old gods. He was not certain that even Laoghaire was safe from it. The druids had reason to worry. In Laoghaire's stronghold, his British wife was busy persuading him to grant the British bishop an audience.

"I have heard such good things about this man of God. They say that he is in constant contact with God through prayer, and that he is wiser than anyone else in the land!" the queen exclaimed.

"They probably say that he has four arms and a tongue made out of fire, too," laughed Laoghaire. "They say a lot of things."

"Yes, but how will you know what is true and what is just talk if you don't invite him to speak to you? You are surely not afraid of this priest and his followers?"

"Of course I'm not afraid of them!"

"Or are you afraid of what the druids will say?" asked the queen slyly. "They would certainly not welcome the competition for your heart, I'm sure."

"I'm not afraid of priests or druids, and my heart is my own," grumbled Laoghaire. "But if it will make you happy then very well, I will invite him to the fortress."

Patrick's companions could not suppress their excitement when they heard about the invitation their leader had received to visit the king in his stronghold.

"This is such a great opportunity to spread the good news!" said Auxilius, who had recently come to Ireland to join in Patrick's work.

"That is true, but this opportunity is not without danger," warned Patrick. "Laoghaire is served by powerful druids, and they will not want him or his household to hear our message. Accepting the true God means turning your back on magic and superstitions."

"I had heard that the druids are very important to King Laoghaire," agreed Lomman gloomily. "They are even responsible for the education of his daughters."

"Remember," said Patrick, "our struggle is not against flesh and blood, but against the dark powers that enslave people. So pray for me as I visit Laoghaire, and pray that he and his household would be ready to accept the truth. But pray for the druids, too."

It was a nervous night for Patrick's followers. The invitation to visit Laoghaire had only included Patrick and a couple of close companions, not his entire group of missionaries, which was now quite large, including Irish Christians as well as workers from Britain and Europe. They could see the fortress on the hill, and make out the lights from its narrow windows, but they had no idea what was going on inside. Was Laoghaire listening eagerly to the good news about Jesus, or was he telling Patrick not to interfere in the traditional religion of his ancestors? What if something Patrick said offended him? Would he have Patrick thrown out, or locked up, or killed on the spot? The group of Christians spent the night in prayer for their leader, asking God to protect him and open the ears of the people who were listening to him.

Eventually, early the next morning, a small group of men could be seen coming down the hill from the fortress.

"It's Patrick!" called Auxilius. "And the others! Look, they are safe!" He and his friends rushed to greet their fellow workers, and find out how the visit had gone. Some of them began cooking up food for breakfast while Patrick and his companions settled themselves to tell the story.

"Thank you for your prayers," Patrick said. "I needed them because I was in real danger!"

"Did Laoghaire assault you? Did he try to have to locked up?"

"No, it was not Laoghaire, it was his druids who tried to kill me. They poisoned my wine cup!" Patrick's companions' faces showed their shock.

"Are you all right?" Auxilius asked.

"I am completely well," Patrick replied. "By the grace of God, I was prevented from drinking the poison, and Laoghaire's druids were revealed as the murderers they are."

"What did the king do?"

"Nothing," said Patrick with a shrug. "I got the impression that he had let them try to poison me, just to see what would happen. Anyway, when the trick didn't work, it made a big impression on him. So much so that he has granted us some of his land to build another church!"

"That's wonderful news, Patrick!" said Auxilius "Do you mean to tell us that the High King Laoghaire has become a Christian?"

"No, I'm afraid not," said Patrick. "He is not ready to give up the traditions of his ancestors, or to accept the truth about the one true God. We can continue to pray for him, however. He is not going to oppose our work, and some members of his household have already become Christians!"

By this time, breakfast was ready. As they ate it, Patrick and his companions talked excitedly about the new opportunity that had opened up for them, being able to tell people about Jesus in Laoghaire's kingdom with his consent and even support.

But if Patrick's companions thought that they were out of danger now, they were wrong. Laoghaire was prepared to hold his druids in check and make sure that they did not attack Patrick and his followers, but other kings and chiefs were less keen on Patrick and his teachings. Patrick was aware of the danger that was constantly in the background. Wherever he or his followers went, he made payments to the local chief for safe passage through the land and for protection from their soldiers, where it was available. But sometimes, even that was not enough.

"Who are those men approaching on horseback?" asked Auxilius one day, as they walked through wild countryside between one village and another. "They look rather well armed. Do you think our bodyguards will be able to tackle them, if they give us any trouble?" As he spoke, Auxilius turned his head to look at the soldiers of the local chief who were following them, and realized they had been betrayed.

"Patrick!" he shouted. "The bodyguards have gone! Look, there they are, running off in the distance. They must have been paid to abandon us. It's a trap!" The party of Christians stopped dead in their tracks and watched the group of heavily armed men thundering down on them. Patrick could feel the panic rising in the group.

"Don't worry," he said, "just pray. Remember that God is in charge, and nothing will happen to us against his will. Trust in God!" That was the last word he was able to utter, for the armed men were right on top of them, swinging clubs at the heads and shoulders of the missionaries. Auxilius threw himself on the ground, getting a knock to his head that made him dizzy. Hooves stamped around him, kicking up muck and stones. His companions cried out in fear and the attackers shouted war cries. He rolled, and bumped into someone, but he couldn't tell who. Someone shouted out, "Stop, come back!" Then it was all over. Auxilius, spitting mud and grass from his mouth, realized that the noise of hooves was fading away and there was no more shouting. Sitting up carefully, his spinning head making him want to be sick, he asked, "What happened?" His companions' stricken faces told him the answer even before one of them spoke.

"They've got him. They've taken Patrick!"

* * *

Patrick had no idea where he was. His captors had ridden so fast through unmarked countryside that he could not possibly guess where they had taken him, and the sun had been behind thick clouds so he could not even say for sure what direction they had traveled in. Now he was tied up in some kind of a roundhouse, with armed men at the door. Patrick knew it was impossible that any of his friends could have followed the kidnappers, even if they had not been injured or killed in the attack. He wondered what his captors planned to do with him. It seemed unlikely that they would sell him as an ordinary slave, now that he was so well known. Perhaps they planned to kill him, or to deliver him to one of his enemies. Was this the end of his mission to Ireland?

Patrick felt alone and vulnerable as night started to fall. He wondered if he would ever see his followers again. He thought about trying to escape, but he knew how dangerous that would be if the ruthless armed men caught him. Instead, he entrusted himself to God.

"Christ is with me, even when I am alone and in the hands of my enemies," he said to himself. "Christ is with me, even in this house. Christ is within me, and Christ surrounds me." Comforted by this thought, Patrick managed to drift off to sleep, and in his sleep God spoke to him in a dream, as he had done before. A voice spoke to him saying, "You shall be with them for two months." It seemed only a moment before Patrick opened his eyes and it was morning.

"I will be with them for only two months," he said, with a smile on his face. The leader of the bandit group was astonished when he stomped in to check on the prisoner and found him beaming pleasantly.

Sure enough, after eight weeks with the surly bunch, moving from place to place without any details about where they were going or why, the leader of the bandits came to speak to Patrick, looking as if he had been chewing nettles.

"There's been a change of plan," he spat. "We're going to let you go. You've obviously got friends in high places, Christian!"

"The very highest place," agreed Patrick. The group set him free on the outskirts of a nearby town, where Patrick was able to ask directions to the nearest Christian church. After he arrived he was eventually reunited with his friends. They were overjoyed to see their leader alive and well.

"I told you that God had a plan," said Patrick. "Who knows, perhaps he will even touch the hearts of those bandits that held me. It seems that he has already changed the heart of whoever was paying them to kidnap me!"

This raid did not turn out to be the last time Patrick and his friends experienced the anger of chiefs and religious leaders who did not want their message to spread. Many times, as the years wore on, enemies attacked Patrick or his followers, trying to kill them or capture them. Sometimes, they succeeded in taking them prisoner, but every time God saved his missionaries from slavery and death. Many times, criminals or the soldiers of hostile chiefs robbed Patrick and his colleagues of whatever they had and left them bruised and beaten. The constant danger did not put the Christians off from their work. Patrick got used to looking out for traps and enemies, trusting God to keep him safe. Patrick, at the very least, used these dangerous situations to spread the good news about Jesus.

It was wearing, always feeling that danger could wait round the next corner, and knowing that so many people wanted him dead or out of the country. Sometimes Patrick felt lonely. He thought about Gaul, and the good friends he had there. It hurt to think that he would never see them again; he would spend the rest of his life on this island. But Patrick knew that this was where he was supposed to be, so he patiently continued the work of spreading the Christian message to Ireland's kings, chiefs, and people. He never guessed that after so many years of hard work he would face a different kind of opposition—this time, from back home!

A Friendship Betrayed

Patrick couldn't help but feel quite pleased. He knew that it was God who was responsible for his success in Ireland, but it was still satisfying to be a big part of it. He had just come back from the baptism of a dozen Irish people who had become Christians, which was wonderful in itself. But when he thought that the man who baptized them was also Irish, and had not known about Jesus until Patrick and his colleagues had arrived, it made it even more special. The church in Ireland was really flourishing, with so many churches that it took weeks to visit them all. The many years of hard work that Patrick and his colleagues had put in were certainly paying off.

Patrick looked fondly at Benignus, walking by his side. This modest and intelligent young man was the son of an Irish chief, and Patrick was training him up to be one of the leaders of the church after he was gone. The British bishop was getting beyond his middle years, and had already started thinking about providing for the Irish church after he died. However, on a day like this, Patrick felt that the Irish church would do very well, with or without him. God had certainly blessed the work he had sent Patrick to do.

Patrick's mood became even lighter when he heard that a letter had arrived for him from Britain. Letters came rarely, since they had to be sent with travelers coming to Ireland, and travel between the two countries was increasingly unsafe. Patrick opened the letter eagerly, hoping to hear news of home or an encouraging message letting him know that the church in Britain was still praying for him and supporting his mission. The contents of the letter, however, were completely different.

Written in stiff and formal language, the document Patrick held in his hand accused him of dishonesty and inappropriate use of church funds. Although it did not say it quite so bluntly, the British church was accusing Patrick of stealing! Patrick's face flushed at the unfairness of it. He had devoted his entire inheritance to this mission, and never once misused the funds that had been entrusted to him. There was no reason given for the suspicion—perhaps the British church was merely wondering what Patrick had done with all the funding it had been sending for years.

The letter was not all bad news, however. Enclosed with the accusation and formal notice that Patrick's case would be tried by the church, was a note from some of the elders of his home church telling Patrick that he did have supporters. Patrick's friend Proditus, who had recommended him for the position of bishop, would plead Patrick's case when the church considered the matter.

The note gave Patrick a little peace. Proditus would surely set the record straight. The problem must just be that the British church did not realize how expensive it was to support church leaders in a land where the churchgoers were so poor, and the distances between populations were so great. Then there were the payments to the chiefs, which were essential for the safety of the workers spreading the Christian message. Patrick's heartbeat was still a bit elevated from the horrible suspicions, but he quickly sat down to write to Proditus, to thank him for his loyalty and to explain in detail the situation in Ireland. He entrusted the letter to a helper to take it to the coast, with some money to pay for its passage on a ship traveling to Britain. The letter would have to pass through many hands and would no doubt take weeks to arrive with Proditus, but Patrick felt better knowing that it was on its way to a friend who would speak up for him against the horrible accusations.

In the meantime, Patrick had to get on with the work as usual. Although he was older now, he was still active. He traveled many miles in all sorts of weather to visit churches and chiefs, to spread the word to those who had not yet heard about Jesus, and to teach and encourage those who had already accepted the message. There were so many churches now, it was difficult to keep count, and it was impossible to count all the Christians! The long hours of work helped to distract Patrick's mind from the mutterings about him in Britain. But still, sometimes, on the long roads between villages, his mind would wander back to the letter. He would then take the matter to God in prayer, asking for help to trust his Heavenly Father, and for forgiveness for giving in to worry.

It was a long time before Patrick heard any more about the accusations against him. Returning from a long journey to baptize some new Christians in another part of Ireland, he was told that there was a letter waiting for him. Patrick was tired from the journey and badly needed to rest, but he did not want to wait any longer to find out how Proditus was getting on with his defense. He asked for the letter to be brought to him. Patrick hoped that the message would tell him that the whole thing had been a misunderstanding and he could forget about it, but he knew that might not be the case, and he prepared himself for the worst.

What he read was worse than the worst. The letter told him that evidence had been produced against Patrick to indicate that he had a history of untrustworthiness. Without going into too much detail, it gave an account of a sin that Patrick had been accused of. Patrick grew pale. Noticing how shaken their leader looked, some of Patrick's priests rushed to get him a stool. Patrick hardly noticed when they helped him to sit down on it. His eyes glazed over as he traveled back through his memory.

This new accusation was true. The sin they mentioned, Patrick had committed. It had been decades earlier, before he was a Christian, when he was only about fifteen and living back in Britain. Patrick was ashamed of it, but he knew that God had forgiven him, as he forgives the sins of everyone who accepts Jesus. That was not what had shaken Patrick to the core. The reason he had grown so pale was that he had only ever told one person about this secret sin, just before he had been ordained as a deacon. No one else knew. And the one person he had told—was Proditus.

Patrick sipped the water that his followers had brought for him and tried to pull himself together, but he could barely keep his emotions in check. He explained to his concerned friends what the letter had said, without going into details about what he was accused of, or of who was responsible for the accusation.

"So it looks as if the case against me is still proceeding, and my defense is not going as well as I had hoped," he concluded, his voice a little more steady now. "I don't know what will happen if the British church decides that I am not a suitable person to lead this mission. I don't know if they will continue to support the mission, if they ask me to return to Britain…"

"R-return to Britain?" stammered Benignus. Patrick had been his spiritual leader since he was a child, and was almost a father to him. He could not imagine life without Patrick.

"I honestly don't know what the outcome will be," said Patrick, trying to sound reassuring, but not really managing. "We must be prepared for whatever comes. We must prepare our hearts to accept God's will. I still believe, however, that God has called me to Ireland for the rest of my life. He has given me no sign to the contrary." He sighed again. "Perhaps the church in Ireland will just have to do without the church in Britain."

"I don't mean to speak out of turn, Patrick," said Secundinus, who had been listening to everything Patrick had said, "but if the British church is unfair and unwise enough to withdraw its support…" Patrick gave him a warning look for his disrespectful tone, but Secundinus carried on: "… then I think the church in Ireland will be perfectly able to continue without it. What you have achieved is amazing!" There were some murmurs of agreement from the others, but Patrick cut them short.

"I have achieved nothing, except what the Lord has granted me. He prepared the work for me to do, and he has produced the fruit. I will not take the credit."

"Yes, of course, but even so," said Secundinus, dismissing Patrick's objections, "look at how the church stands in Ireland now. There are churches all over the island, with thousands upon thousands of believers. Many young people have begun to form communities where they dedicate their lives to Christ—even the sons and daughters of chiefs and kings! I know that most of the Christians here are too poor to offer much support, but there are also the nobility who offer such expensive gifts!"

"And I have never accepted those gifts!" said Patrick, struggling up from his stool. "I have always refused personal financial gifts, even when the givers begged me to accept them—and even though my elders in the British church thought that I should accept them, to support my ministry! I never take even the smallest gift for myself, so that there can't be even a hint of bribery. The only things I have ever accepted have been land and resources for the churches we have set up, never anything for myself!" Patrick finished his vehement speech and sank back on to his stool, speaking more wearily now.

"The British church *knows* my attitude to gifts, and that I would never accept anything that compromised my ministry. How can they possibly question my integrity now, after so many years of hard service, away from my home, my family, my friends?" He shook his head sadly. There was nothing more to say. Secundinus laid his hand on Patrick's shoulder and after a few moments, some of the other Christians began to pray quietly. They spent the evening in prayer until the need for sleep overcame the turmoil of their minds.

Patrick had expected his sleep to be disturbed by the stressful matter on his mind, but in fact he sank into a very deep sleep, and in the darkness of his dreams, God spoke to him once again. There was a document in front of Patrick's face. He couldn't exactly read it, but in his dream he knew it was in some way dishonorable, like a slanderous accusation. Patrick felt downhearted, looking at the document, but then he heard a voice say, "We are not pleased to see the face of the chosen one deprived of his good name." Patrick knew it was God speaking. The voice came again: "Whoever touches you touches the apple of my eye."

When they went to greet their leader the following morning, Patrick's followers were surprised to see him looking calm and confident. The agitation of the previous day had entirely gone, and the flinty look of determination that was so characteristic of him had returned to Patrick's face. Secundinus could not conceal his astonishment.

"Surely you can't have received word in the night from Britain?" he asked. "We would have heard if a messenger had come in!"

"I've had word from a much more important place," Patrick said. "God spoke to me in the night." He told Secundinus and the others about his dream with the document, and what God had said to him.

"I realize now that I was wrong to worry about my good name, or what the church in Britain thinks of me, or even whether they will continue to support our mission," explained Patrick. "This mission is God's. He has chosen us to spread the good news about his Son to the people of Ireland, and that is what we must do, until he tells us otherwise, or until we have no breath left in our bodies. Now let's get ready—we have work to do!"

Under Attack

It was a beautiful day. A gentle breeze blew off the sea, and the sun shone kindly down through light cloud. The dark emerald green of the grass contrasted with the bleached white clothes of the candidates. It was the perfect day for a baptism, and the priest in charge smiled as he called the next candidate forward.

A shy young girl stepped toward him. She smiled back as she repeated after the priest the words that confirmed her faith in one God—Father, Son, and Holy Spirit. The priest dipped his finger into the little jug of oil he was carrying, and made the sign of the cross on the girl's forehead to show that her journey into membership of the Christian church was complete. He congratulated her briefly, but there were still several candidates waiting. With a gesture, he asked the girl to step to the side, and beckoned the next candidate. The girl went and stood among the large crowd of baptized Christians, and those nearest her offered their congratulations too. The sun shone on the oily crosses on their foreheads.

The priest had moved on to a dark-haired young man, and because he was concentrating on asking the candidate to repeat the appropriate words, at first he did not realize what was happening. He thought that the noise at the back was people chatting or joking. He wondered if he would have to ask them to settle down, or if the importance of the occasion would make them quieten down themselves. It wasn't until he had finished with the dark-haired young man and called forward another candidate that he realized something more serious was going on. Heads had started to turn, to find out where the noise was coming from. There was shouting, and it was growing louder, and closer. With an apology to the remaining candidates, the priest started forward through the crowd to find out what was causing the disturbance.

As he drew nearer, he heard screams as the people nearest the back started to see clearly what was coming. No longer apologetic, the priest pushed his way through, in time to see a Pictish war band descending on the crowd of newly baptized Christians, swords drawn. Their skin was painted in weird patterns and their red mouths were open in obscene war cries. The priest raised his hand automatically in a gesture of "stop", but there was no stopping this band. A slash from the sword threw the priest to one side, and the armed men set about their awful work amongst the screaming victims.

Everywhere, white robes turned dark with blood as the Picts cut their way through the newly baptized group. Some tried to fight back, but they were unarmed, and unprepared. Others ran. Soon a pattern started to emerge. The men were stabbed or slashed and left to die, but the women were grabbed alive. Groups of them were tied hand and foot and dragged to the side, struggling and weeping. Within less than an hour, the Picts were dragging their reluctant captives away, leaving the happy baptismal scene churned up with mud and blood. The only Christians left behind were dead.

It wasn't long before the news reached Patrick. At first, it was just a third-hand report that something terrible had happened at the baptism, with no details. By the following morning, however, some of the survivors were brought to Patrick to tell what they knew. As they described the awful scene they had run from—Christians wounded and dying, women rounded up like cattle—tears started in Patrick's eyes. He had met all of these converts. He had been the one who had spoken to them about their faith, and authorized their baptism. He had looked forward to welcoming them as a father into the growing Irish church, once they had completed the baptism ceremony. He thought of the familiar names and faces—some dead, some taken, all of them so full of life and optimism yesterday, and the pain he was feeling grew to a burning anger.

"We must do something!" he cried to his followers. "We can't let these brigands and pirates kill and kidnap our people. Who is in charge of this raiding band? Who do they answer to? Perhaps we know the king who commands them, and can use our influence to get them released."

"I don't think that will work," said Iserninus. "The bandits were Pictish warriors from the mainland, not from Ireland. And according to the local people, who have been raided before, they are commanded by Coroticus of Strathclyde."

Coroticus. Patrick knew the name. Coroticus had been a minor leader during Patrick's childhood, but now the Roman army was gone, and so far there were no signs that it was coming back. In the absence of Roman leadership from the mainland, men who had private soldiers under their command had started to turn themselves into little kings, ruling tiny kingdoms. Some of them offered peace and security to the people in their region. Others just spent their time raiding and plundering. It looked as if Coroticus thought Ireland, across the sea from his little kingdom, was fair game, and had sent his hired thugs to take some prisoners that he could sell as slaves. Patrick knew something else about Coroticus, too, something that filled him with terrible anger.

"Coroticus is a Christian! Or at least he claims to be. He is a Roman citizen, just like I am! How dare he attack Christians, in the middle of a baptism ceremony? He is acting worse than any barbarian!" He looked around. "Go and find Benignus," he requested. "He is a young man, fit and active, but also a reliable priest. Find other young priests too—whoever is quick and strong, and is able to set out on a journey immediately. Benignus must go to the raiding party, accompanied by the others for safety. If he is quick, he will reach them before they set sail. Coroticus must be made to understand how terrible his actions were! I will appeal to him through my messengers as a fellow Christian, and as a bishop, and make him release those poor girls! Hurry!" Secundinus did as he was asked, and rushed out the door. Patrick sat down to wait, spending the time in urgent prayer until Benignus, panting, appeared through the doorway.

"Benignus! Thank you for coming so quickly. You have heard about what happened yesterday, of course?" Benignus nodded silently. It looked as if he might have been crying.

"The attackers work for Coroticus of Strathclyde. You must go to him, imploring and commanding him to release the prisoners. Explain that the women he captured and the men he had killed were newly baptized Christians —they are his brothers and sisters! Please hurry, Benignus. Take the other young priests I have sent for. Borrow horses from wherever you can find them, and run on your own feet if you can't, but find this war band before they leave our shores and take our baptized sisters with them!" He squeezed the young man's hand with a fierce pressure. Benignus squeezed Patrick's hand back in reassurance.

"I will do whatever I can to reach them before it is too late," he promised.

The next day passed anxiously. Patrick and the others held services of prayer for the captives, and started the horrible business of burying the bodies of the murdered men and boys. There were a lot of bodies to bury. As each hour of the day wore on, Patrick felt both fear and hope—hope that Benignus and the others would return with good news, and fear that they would not return at all. But he knew that the matter was out of his hands, and in the hands of God. Worrying would do no good; he could only trust. Time and again, he tore his mind away from worrying about the captives, and back to the task of dealing with the dead.

Eventually, a weary and forlorn Benignus made his way back to the settlement, accompanied by other footsore young men. Patrick scanned the group anxiously. Everyone was accounted for who had gone to deliver the message, but there were no extra travelers with them on the way back—no released captives. Benignus saw Patrick's questioning face as he approached to greet him, and shook his head.

"We didn't get them, Patrick. We found the captives, but the raiders weren't interested in what we had to say. They don't care about God's law, or human laws. They just laughed in our faces." Patrick put his arm round the young man, who was like a son to him.

"Thank you for trying, all of you. We couldn't just sit back and do nothing. But tell me, did Coroticus himself laugh in your faces? Did he have no respect for the authority of the church?"

"Coroticus wasn't there," chipped in one of the other priests who had made the journey. "He had just sent his hired men to do his dirty business for him."

"He wasn't there? What, not in Ireland at all?" asked Secundinus, who had come to hear the news. The young priest shook his head. "Well, in that case," continued Secundinus, with a trace of hope, "Coroticus himself probably doesn't know anything about the baptism, or that the new prisoners are Christians—not if he's back in Britain."

"He must be told!" exclaimed Patrick. "This is shocking behavior for a Roman citizen, and a supposed Christian, even if he did not know that his victims would be Christians! But perhaps he will repent when he hears, or perhaps he will respond to discipline. The church must make him answer for his crimes!"

At that, a shadow passed across Patrick's face, deepening the already deep wrinkles. His companions could guess the cause of it. The church that Coroticus should answer to was the British church, but the relationship between Patrick and the church back home was not good. Nothing had ever come of the investigation into Patrick years before; perhaps there was too little evidence either way. Patrick had never been recalled to Britain—but his name had never been fully cleared, either.

It wasn't just that making Patrick look pessimistic, however. Even now, decades after his decision to follow God's call to Ireland, Patrick remembered the reaction of the church elders, and especially the other people in his community. They had not thought that the Irish deserved a missionary to show them how to be saved from their sins. It didn't seem likely that people would have changed their minds now. Could the British church really be trusted to deal with Coroticus for kidnapping Irish Christians, if they didn't think that Ireland even mattered to God?

Patrick was silent for a long moment. Then he raised his head and spoke with decision.

"I will write a letter. This letter will be addressed to Coroticus, but it will also be an open letter, to all the Christians in Britain, to anyone who has anything to do with Coroticus. I will explain the terrible thing that was done at his command, the way women were taken like possessions to be passed round, the way young men, barely grown, were killed in their baptismal robes! I will let everyone know what Coroticus really is, and whoever is prepared to trade with him, eat with him, even talk with him after that—let them answer to their own conscience!"

"Do you think he will take any notice, Patrick?" asked Secundinus "We have no troops, we don't even have any authority over him. You are bishop of Ireland, not Strathclyde."

"God has authority over him," answered Patrick grimly. "It is to God that he will have to answer for his behavior, for his greed and violence. That is what I will make clear to him. Make sure I am not disturbed for the next few hours." Saying this, Patrick ducked his head and entered the low doorway of the building he had come from, and gathered together his writing materials. The others quietly left him to it.

Patrick sat by the doorway to use the light from the sun. Dipping his quill pen carefully in the inkwell, not wanting to waste precious parchment, he started to compose the letter in his simple, imperfect Latin.

"I am Patrick, an uneducated sinner, established as bishop here in Ireland. I would not have wanted to use such harsh words as these, but I am driven by the zeal of God, and roused by the truth of Christ. I am not writing to my fellow citizens, or holy Roman citizens, but to people who are fellow citizens of demons, because of their wicked deeds! People steeped in the blood of innocent Christians!"

Patrick drew a deep breath and composed himself. It would be easy to get carried away. Filling his pen with ink once again, he started to explain exactly what had happened the day before. His eyes filled with tears as he considered all the victims, those who were dead and those who might suffer a fate worse than death, depending on what their captors decided to do with them. As best he could, Patrick conveyed the horror of what the "ravening wolves" sent from Coroticus had done.

"What kind of hope can you have left in God?" Patrick appealed to the warlord in his scratchy pen.

"Even if you're surrounded by flatterers, God will judge you! 'Do not covet' and 'do not murder.'" Patrick wrote the familiar words of the Bible from memory. "'What good will it do anyone to gain the whole world but lose their soul?'"

Patrick couldn't be sure if his letter would ever reach Coroticus, or if he would pay any attention, but he appealed to anyone else who might read it and who had contact with Coroticus. Surely no Christian would have anything to do with him when they knew what he had done? Patrick intended to make sure that people did know. He closed his letter with an appeal to everyone whose hands the letter might pass through, that they would read it out and pass it on until it reached the ears of Coroticus himself, in the hope that he would be sorry for his actions and order the release of the women.

Eventually, his back sore from leaning over the table and his hand stiff from writing, Patrick got up, folded the letter, and walked outside to find a younger man to entrust it to.

"Take this to the coast," he said to the young Christian. "Put it on the first ship heading to Strathclyde, or anywhere near there. Here is money for its passage. Don't seal it – I want everyone to read it."

The young man hurried away, and Secundinus, who had seen him pass on the letter, walked over to Patrick.

"So it's done," he said.

"It is done."

"Do you think it will work? Do you think Coroticus will release the women and ask for forgiveness?" Patrick shrugged, the action showing all the weariness of his long and hard life in Ireland.

"I don't know, Secundinus. I can only hope and pray that it does. And we must pray for the captives. They are in God's hands. But I knew another young man, long ago, who was a captive in God's hands—and he, for one, discovered that God is faithful."

Going Home

Patrick watched the white crests dancing on the high waves as he stared out to sea. The stiff wind that was blowing the spume about threatened to buffet the old man off his feet. Across the water lay Britain. On a clear day, it was visible, but this was not a clear day, and anyway, Patrick's eyes were not as sharp as they had once been. He was now in his seventies and he doubted if he would see another winter through. He knew in his heart that he would never go to Britain again, the land he had left half a lifetime ago to serve in Ireland. Patrick's thoughts drifted back to his first journey across the water, when he had been only sixteen. He remembered how scared he had been, the hot tears in his eyes, his tongue dry in his mouth. It had seemed like the end of the world, like the end of his life. That ignorant, sinful young boy could never have dreamed of the plans that God had for him. The end of his world had been just the beginning of his new life.

With a heavy sigh of weariness, Patrick turned back inland. He had come out here to pray, but if he stayed too long the young priests would start to get worried about their elderly leader. It was good to have bright young people who were concerned about him, but Patrick knew, that when his time came to die, they would manage perfectly well without him. Already he was getting too weak to make as many journeys as he had, and the new young priests—he still thought of them that way, even though some were in their forties or fifties—did most of the work of looking after the Christian community, which now numbered in the thousands.

Patrick thought about all the faces he had seen come and go over the decades. Young Benignus, who gave him so much joy. No longer such a young man, he was a worthy person to step into Patrick's shoes when the moment came. More sadly, Patrick thought of Secundinus, his good friend who had tramped the paths and hills of Ireland with him more times than Patrick could remember. He had died a few years ago, an old man himself, and although there were many other helpers and friends, Patrick felt the loss of one who had been with him in this mission since the beginning. Patrick called to mind his mother, crying her eyes out over him leaving, his father, his face etched with years of worry. They were long dead too, of course, and Patrick thought it was likely that he would soon be going to join them. With that in mind, he had started a little project that he intended to complete before he died.

Patrick walked down the hill toward the building that stood on the land Dichu had given him right at the start of his mission, and had a peaceful feeling of having come full circle. The members of the Christian community on this spot saw Patrick coming toward them, and waved a greeting. One of them came up to him to offer his arm, and Patrick, whose knees only seemed to get stiffer, was not too proud to take it.

"Are you hungry? Should I fetch you some lunch?" asked the young Irishman. "I think there's some stew and some fresh bread in the kitchen."

"Thank you, but I'm not hungry just now," answered Patrick. "I think I shall do some more writing. Could you help me to move my table to the doorway, where I can see better?"

"Of course." Everyone knew that Patrick had started writing a document, the story of what God had done in his life, and in Ireland through him, but it was not finished and he had not let anyone see it so far.

Patrick settled himself at the table, letting the weak sunlight do what it could to warm him. He picked up his pen and continued the document he was writing— partly the story of his life, partly the story of God's work in Ireland, and partly a confession of Patrick's faith in God the Father, Jesus the Son, and the Holy Spirit, to help others to hold to the faith after he had gone.

Patrick looked at what he had written up to then, with all its little mistakes and corrections, and wished once again that he had paid more attention to his lessons as a boy. If only he had known then that the soft life of childhood and education would not go on forever, and how much he would regret his ignorance once it was too late! But there was nothing he could do about it now; he just had to manage the best he could with the abilities he had. All of Ireland was his witness to how faithful God had been in using Patrick's abilities, however limited.

"I have been thinking about writing for some time," Patrick scratched carefully on the page with his quill pen, "but I have put it off until now. I was afraid of how people would criticize me, because my weak Latin makes it obvious that I haven't studied since I was a boy. But my gratitude will not let me keep silent! I ought to shout out my thanks because God chose me for this task of bringing the love of Christ to the people of Ireland, even though I was not wise or well educated.

"So all of you eloquent speakers reading this, be amazed at what God can do, even through someone like me! Because of my faith in God the Father, Son, and Holy Spirit, I spoke about him everywhere. I never gave in to fear, no matter what the danger, and when I die I will leave behind thousands of brothers, sisters, and children in Christ—people who came to know Jesus because God used me! I faced lots of dangers and problems in Ireland, and I was taken prisoner many times, but I could never have imagined, when I was young, just how much God would bless me in this place, with these people!"

Patrick paused from his writing, and rested his hand on the table. It was easy to write about how grateful he was to God, because it was true. His teenage self, kidnapped and scared, would never have understood; but God had given Patrick a real love for the people of this island at the end of the world, and the people had returned Patrick's love. He still had colleagues from Britain and other parts of the Roman Empire, but almost everyone in the Irish church—thousands and thousands of people—had never even been to the Roman Empire. God's kingdom truly extended even to the ends of the earth.

Patrick picked up the pen and continued his work, describing the course of his life, and all the things God had done through him. Sometimes it was painful, when he had to talk about the way people criticized him for going to Ireland, or the way Proditus had betrayed him when the British church had suspected Patrick of being dishonest. Patrick knew it was important to tell the truth as well as he could remember it, though, and not take out the painful bits to make a more uplifting story. He was strict with himself, examining his conscience for every statement he wrote, checking that it was really the truth. He had to admit that he would love to visit his relatives in Britain again, or to go and visit his friends in Gaul, but he knew that Jesus Christ had commanded him to come back to Ireland for the rest of his life—and it was Jesus who helped him to resist the temptation to give up and leave when things were hard.

"Even now," Patrick wrote, "I know that any day I could be murdered, or betrayed, or made a slave again. But I am not afraid, because I believe in Almighty God, who reigns everywhere." Patrick knew that this was true. If his eventful life had taught him anything, it was that God was with him wherever he went, and whatever happened to him. He was never alone.

"I never had any reason to return to Ireland after I finally managed to escape, except to tell the good news of God," Patrick wrote, summing up the story of his life. "Anything I have achieved has been the gift of God. And this is my confession before I die."

Patrick laid down his pen, breathing out with relief. It could still do with some corrections, and he would have to write it out again before it was really fit for people to read, but at least it was done. He had told his story, and given to God the glory that he deserved for everything he had done for Patrick, and for Ireland.

Patrick was right to think that the end of his life was approaching. On the seventeenth day of March, he died in the land he had made his own. He was an old man who had not visited his homeland in over thirty years when God took him to his heavenly home. Patrick's followers buried him in the land that Dichu had given him to build a church—the very place that Patrick had first started his mission in Ireland. There were many places in Ireland that Patrick had loved, and where he had built churches, but this was certainly one of them. Patrick had dined with kings and baptized princes and princesses, but as the "uneducated sinner" would have wished, his tomb and his burial were simple, with no fuss. Still, Patrick's followers remembered the date of his death and passed it down to generation after generation, along with the stories of what Patrick had done in Ireland, so that he would not be forgotten.

Across the sea to the south, in Europe, the Roman Empire continued to crumble. The troops that had been withdrawn from protecting Britain were never coming back. New, self-made rulers seized power, and the country broke up into pocket-sized kingdoms. Refined Roman customs and education became, like Patrick's childhood, just a faded memory. Settlers, traders, and marauders arrived from the east and started to take over most of Britain, bringing with them their pagan beliefs and culture, and a new language—English. However, in Ireland, the Christian church that Patrick had dedicated his life to continued to flourish. Christian communities passed down education about God and the Bible, and even passed on the study of Latin. Patrick could never have imagined just how much God would reward his obedience in returning to Ireland to tell the people there the good news about Jesus; but one hundred years after Patrick's death, missionaries from Ireland would cross the narrow sea to take the same good news back to Britain.

Thinking Further Topics

Chapter One – Kidnapped!
When Patrick was captured and sold into slavery, along with thousands of others, he must have felt very scared and helpless. The fact that kidnap was against the law didn't stop the raiders, who knew they could get away with it. Even today, usually in poorer parts of the world, many people are captured or tricked and made to work as slaves. Spend a few moments praying for modern-day slaves, that they would be rescued, and that they would know the peace of God during their captivity.

Chapter Two – Six Years a Slave
When Patrick refused to take part in a pagan ritual of friendship, it could have blown his only chance of getting a ship back to Britain, but he refused anyway. Are there times when you are tempted to pretend you're not a Christian, or to do something you know is wrong, so that you can fit in? How might you avoid these situations, or find the courage to stand out?

Chapter Three – The Longest Way Home
The storm that hit Patrick's ship ruined his plans for getting home quickly, but he was still able to trust in God, even though he didn't understand God's plans. What are your most important plans or hopes? Are you prepared to trust God, even if he has different ideas for you?

Chapter Four – Called by God
Being called back to Ireland was the last thing that Patrick expected. It was such a strange idea, and communicated in such an unusual way (in his dream) that he knew it must be from God, but still he prayed to check that he was on the right track. If you feel that God is calling you to do something or go somewhere, who could you talk to for advice on testing whether you are right?

Chapter Five – To Go or Not To Go
Some people thought that Patrick should not go to Ireland as a missionary because the Irish did not deserve to be told about Jesus. Have you ever heard anyone say that some people don't deserve God's forgiveness? Have you ever said something like that yourself? Or do you believe that God wants everyone to repent and be saved (2 Peter 3:9)?

Chapter Six – Back to Ireland
Almost as soon as he landed back in Ireland, Patrick met someone who was keen to hear about Jesus Christ.

God prepares people's hearts in advance to make them ready to hear the good news about Jesus. If you got talking to someone who is ready to learn about Jesus, what would you tell them?

Chapter Seven – Fighting Against the Darkness

Being a Christian can be dangerous. Patrick was opposed by religious leaders—druids—and some political leaders, and was often attacked or captured. There are many places in the world today where it is dangerous to be a Christian. You can find out more details, and points to pray for, on websites such as Open Doors.

Chapter Eight – A Friendship Betrayed

Being betrayed or let down by a friend can be one of the hardest things to deal with. Even so, it is important to have Christian friends, and to confess our sins to each other (James 5:16). Is there any sin that you are holding against someone? Pray to God to help you forgive and forget.

Chapter Nine – Under Attack

Christians are not always good examples of Christlike behavior. They say good things about Jesus but then don't back that up by their lifestyle. Coroticus, with his slave raids, was a pretty extreme example of this, but is there anything you do that conflicts with what you believe in?

Chapter Ten – Going Home

Patrick was grateful for everything that God had done in Ireland through him, and wanted future generations to know about it. Imagine you are old, looking back on your life. What would you like to be able to tell people about how you served God during your time on earth?

Historical Note

Patrick wrote two documents that still survive, the *Letter to Coroticus* and his *Confession*. Both give some details about his life. However, it's very hard to piece together the course of Patrick's life because while he mentioned the things that he did and events that happened to him, he doesn't give much indication of when, where, or in what order these things took place.

In writing this book I have had to put events into a logical order, which may or may not be correct—for example, the raid by Coroticus may have taken place before Patrick was accused by the church, rather than after. We just don't know.

Another thing we don't know from Patrick's writings are the names of his companions and the people he met in Ireland. The only names Patrick gives, apart from his own, are his father Calpurnius, grandfather Potitus, and Coroticus. The names of his companions in this book are not made up, but are taken from sources written later about Patrick. They are less reliable than Patrick's own documents, so I have only used the names that are found in the earliest and best sources—people like Secundinus (also known as Seachnall), Auxilius, Iserninus, and Benignus. Patrick also never gave the name of the friend who betrayed him. I have given him the name Proditus because it means 'traitor' in Latin.

People who are familiar with the story of Patrick may wonder why I have not included the famous stories about him casting snakes out of Ireland and explaining the Trinity using a shamrock. The reason is that these stories only started being told much later and are probably legend rather than fact. There probably weren't any snakes to drive out, and although Patrick could have used a shamrock to explain theology, we don't have any firm evidence that he did.

Here are some other things that we can't be sure of:

We don't know where Patrick studied, although it was probably Gaul (France) and we don't know that his companions from his studies ever visited his home, but there was a delegation from Gaul in 429, led by Germanus of Auxerre, to combat the heresy of the British monk Pelagius, and this might be when Patrick returned to his home.

We don't know that Patrick sent Benignus to the soldiers of Coroticus, but he says it was a good priest that he had taught from his boyhood, so it is fairly likely.

We can't be sure that Patrick and his companions preached the gospel to High King Laoghaire and his family, but later sources say he did, and the dates in the Irish annals say that he was High King when Patrick arrived in Ireland, in which case it is likely they would have been in contact.

We don't know exactly what the British church accused Patrick of, but since he points out in his *Confession* that he never accepted even the smallest gift and explains all about his payments to kings and chiefs, it seems likely that it was something to do with money. Patrick never says what the outcome of the investigation was, although he obviously continued his work as bishop in Ireland. He also never says what effect, if any, his letter to Coroticus had.

However, we do know that Patrick was kidnapped at age sixteen and taken to Ireland, where he was a slave for six years and was shipwrecked on the way home. He was recalled to Ireland by the dream about Victoricus, and spent some time studying beforehand. He then spent many years establishing churches and preaching the gospel in Ireland. During this time he was accused of something by the British church (and his friend, who was supposed to defend him, brought up a childhood sin instead), and Coroticus's forces attacked a baptism and killed and captured many Christians. I have tried to remain as faithful as possibly to what we actually know about Patrick, without leaving too many gaps.

Main Sources

Patrick, *The Confession of St Patrick* (translated by Ludwig Bieler), Christian Classics Ethereal Library (http://www.ccel.org/ccel/patrick/confession.html), accessed 2015.

Patrick, *A Letter to the Soldiers of Coroticus* (translated by Padraig McCarthy), Royal Irish Academy (http://www.confessio.ie/etexts/epistola_english#01), accessed 2015.

J. B. Bury, *Ireland's Saint: The Essential Biography of St Patrick*, Paraclete Press, 2008.

Michael A. G. Haykin, *Patrick of Ireland: His Life and Impact*, Christian Focus Publications, 2014.

Quotes and Paraphrases from Patrick's Works

Chapter Two
"You will soon return to your home country" and "Look, your ship is ready!" (*Confession* 17)

Chapter Three
"Holy man, we beg you to come and walk among us again!" (*Confession* 23)

Chapter Four
"He who gave his life for you, he is the one who speaks within you." (*Confession* 24)

Chapter Eight
"We have seen with displeasure the face of the chosen one divested of his good name ... He who touches you, touches the apple of my eye." (*Confession* 29)

Chapter Nine
"I am Patrick, yes a sinner and indeed untaught; yet I am established here in Ireland where I profess myself

bishop ... I never would have wanted these harsh words to spill from my mouth; I am not in the habit of speaking so sharply. Yet now I am driven by the zeal of God, Christ's truth has aroused me ... I am not addressing my own people, nor my fellow citizens of the holy Romans, but those who are now become citizens of demons by reason of their evil works ... bloody men who have steeped themselves in the blood of innocent Christians." (*Letter to the Soldiers of Coroticus*, 1-2)

"What kind of hope can you have left in God? Can you still trust someone who says he agrees with you? Do you listen still to all those flatterers who surround you? God alone will judge." (*Letter to the Soldiers of Coroticus*, 14)

Chapter Ten

"And therefore, for some time I have thought of writing, but I have hesitated until now, for truly, I feared to expose myself to the criticism of men ... After hardships and such great trials, after captivity, after many years, he [gave] me so much favor in these people, a thing which in the time of my youth I neither hoped for nor imagined." (*Confession*, 9-15)

"Daily I expect to be murdered or betrayed or reduced to slavery if the occasion arises. But I fear nothing, because of the promises of heaven; for I have cast myself into the hands of Almighty God, who reigns everywhere." (*Confession*, 55)

"I never had any reason, except the gospel and his promises, ever to have returned to that nation from which I had previously escaped with difficulty ... Any trivial thing that I achieved or may have expounded that was pleasing to God ... it would have been the gift of God. And this is my confession before I die." (*Confession* 61-2)

Quotes and Paraphrases from the Bible

Chapter Four

"Christ Jesus ... is at the right hand of God and is also interceding for us" (Romans 8:34).

"The Spirit helps us in our weakness. We do not know what we ought to pray for, but the Spirit himself intercedes for us with groans that words cannot express" (Romans 8:26).

Chapter Five

"But God chose the foolish things of the world to shame the wise; God chose the weak things of the world to shame the strong" (1 Corinthians 1:27).

Chapter Seven

"For our struggle is not against flesh and blood, but against the rulers, against the authorities, against the powers of this dark world and against the spiritual forces of evil in the heavenly realms" (Ephesians 6:12).

Chapter Nine

"You shall not murder" (Deuteronomy 5:17).

"You shall not covet … anything that belongs to your neighbor" (Deuteronomy 5:21).

Patrick of Ireland Timeline

The following is the first chapter from
K.C. Murdarasi's first book on the life of
Augustine: The Truth Seeker
ISBN: 978-1-78191-296-6

A Brush with Death

Augustine swirled water around his clay cup, listening to the gentle sloshing noise. He swirled it harder, making some of the glistening water splash over the side of the cup and fall onto his bare knees and dusty feet. Is this what the sea is like? he wondered, closing his eyes as he tried to imagine a cup of water big enough to separate Africa, where he lived, from Italy, the center of the Roman Empire. It must be scary to cross it! Augustine had never seen the sea, but he was curious about it. The countryside around his villa was covered with olive groves and fir trees and fields of wheat as far as the eye could see. He knew that somewhere, far away to the north, lay the Mediterranean Sea—"Our Sea" as Romans called it because the Roman Empire stretched the whole way around the edge. Augustine had never been further than Thagaste, the town where he lived.

It wasn't just the sea Augustine was curious about. He was interested in plants and birds and animals. In his spare time he liked to wander the countryside with his friends, chasing lizards and birds, and sometimes watching the birds catch the lizards. He had just begun flicking at the water with his fingers, imagining tiny ships tossed about in his stormy cup, when a slave came into the courtyard to call him.

"Master Augustine, it's time to go to school."

"No-o!" groaned Augustine. For a wild moment he thought about running away and hiding in the olive groves until school had finished, but he knew it was no use. His father, Patrick, would find out and beat him, and then he would get sent back to school and the teacher would beat him. Plus, his mother, Monica, would give him one of her disappointed looks, and that was almost worse than a beating. Augustine loved his mother, and he wanted to make her proud of him, but even for her he couldn't pretend to enjoy school. The slave said again, "Master Augustine!"

Sighing, Augustine got up to follow her, pouring his little sea onto the dusty soil of the courtyard as he went.

Monica was a Christian, and even though her husband Patrick was a pagan, he had allowed his wife to bring up Augustine and his brother and sisters as Christians. Augustine said his prayers as his mother had taught him, and every time he prayed he asked God not to let him be beaten at school any more, but it never seemed to work. He would forget his lesson or spell something wrongly, and the teacher would cane him. It happened most of all in Greek classes. Augustine hated Greek! It was bad enough having to learn how to read and write in Latin, his own language, but reading and writing in Greek was impossible!

Augustine would have been happy to make sacrifices to his father's gods, too, if he thought it would help— to mighty Saturn and the Heavenly Goddess—but he knew that they were just stories, not real gods. Even Patrick, who was supposed to believe in them, wasn't especially careful about remembering to sacrifice to them.

Augustine tried to look casual as he walked from his family villa into the town of Thagaste. The school was in an old building near the small forum, or central square. The classroom walls were covered in crumbling plaster and scribbles on the walls from generations of boys. The teacher was already talking so Augustine slipped in quietly and sat down next to one of his friends. That was one good thing about school—he had made a lot of friends.

"What is the lesson about?" he asked in a whisper.

"Dido and Aeneas, from Virgil's Aeneid," replied the other boy. Augustine smiled. This was the only bit of his lessons that he actually liked, the stories from ancient legends. Already he knew bits of the poem the Aeneid by heart and would recite the poetry to himself to enjoy its rhythm. The story of Dido was so sad that it made him want to cry, but it was a nice feeling too. The teacher was telling them about each word in the passage, explaining what type of word it was and why Virgil had chosen it, but Augustine was hardly listening to that. He was thinking about poor Dido left alone in Africa while Aeneas, who was sort

133

of her husband, sailed away to Italy because his destiny awaited him there. It seemed far too short a time before the teacher closed the book and said,

"We will resume Virgil tomorrow. Just now, we will move on to the study of Greek." Augustine put his head in his hands and groaned quietly.

* * *

"Augustine! Augustine, why are you still in bed? You must get up and go to school," called Monica from the corridor outside her son's bedroom. She knew that he hated his Greek lessons, but he was getting on so well with Latin literature and speeches that for many months now he had not begged her to take him out of school, as he used to do. She was surprised that he was still in his bedroom when it was time to go into Thagaste. She pushed back the curtain to the bedroom.

"Augustine?" He was still in bed. Even in the dim light Monica could see that something was wrong. The bedroom was warm but Augustine was shivering. Quickly, she pushed back the shutters from the window. In the daylight she could see that her son was very pale and his forehead was covered in sweat. She brushed back the hair from his forehead.

"Augustine? What's the matter?"

"Mother? Don't feel well. Cold."

Monica ran to the door. "Paula! Send out for the doctor!" she called to her slave. "Augustine is very sick."

The doctor came within an hour, but he did not bring good news.

"This is a very serious fever," he told Monica and Patrick. "I have seen it before. His temperature will reach a peak in a day or two. Then, one of two things will happen. Either the fever will break and he will get well, although he will still feel weak for a while. Or the fever will not break, and the illness will kill him. I must warn you, this is the more likely outcome. You should summon a priest."

Monica turned to Patrick, buried her head in his shoulder and wept for a few moments. Then she took a deep breath and pulled herself together.

"Thank you for your advice, Doctor. Our steward will see to your payment. I will go immediately to Father Crispus and ask him to come." She hurried away, leaving Patrick to see the doctor out, and returned half an hour later with Father Crispus, the local Christian priest. Crispus was a simple man, without much education, and whose Greek was no better than Augustine's, but he was kind and he did his best to teach the people of Thagaste about Jesus and the Bible. Now he spent the afternoon with Augustine, talking to him about Heaven and Hell and the sayings of Jesus. Augustine was very sick but he managed to confess his sins and declare his faith in Jesus through chattering teeth. The priest prayed over the boy, and turned to leave.

"B-baptized. I want to b-be b-baptized!" shivered Augustine. He looked from his mother to the priest.

The two adults looked at each other, but Augustine couldn't tell what they were thinking.

"I'll talk to Father Crispus about it," said Monica, and they left the bedroom. Outside, Monica and the priest talked in hushed voices.

"Do you think it's a good idea, Father?"

"Yes, I think so. I realize that the boy doesn't have much understanding of the faith, but you wouldn't want him to die unbaptized, would you?"

"Of course not!" Monica replied. "But, what if he lives?" The priest nodded sympathetically. He knew why Monica was hesitating. Many people believed that sins committed after baptism were more serious than those committed before baptism. If Augustine lived, he would surely commit some sins in the future —perhaps God would not forgive them? Crispus was no expert and he was not sure if Monica's belief was right. To check, though, would mean asking the bishop, who was out of town. Even if he sent him a letter the reply might not come for several days or weeks. Augustine did not have that long.

"I tell you what, we'll leave it for the time being. If Augustine gets worse and you think he won't make it, send someone to call me at any hour of the day or night. I will come immediately."

"Thank you, Father," said Monica, dabbing her eyes.

Augustine's fever got worse all evening. More than once Monica nearly sent for the priest, but then her son would seem to be more peaceful again and she hesitated. Finally, in the early hours of the morning, she was sure the end had come. Augustine had stopped moaning and shivering. Now he was convulsing, his legs and arms jerking around horribly. His breath came and went with a strange wheezing sound.

"Paula!" Monica screamed. "Send Marcus to get Father Crispus!" She sat holding her son by the shoulders for what felt like hours but was only a few minutes, until eventually he stopped thrashing about and started breathing normally. Monica's scream had woken Patrick, who came into his son's bedroom.

"Is he …?" Patrick couldn't finish the question, and Monica did not know how to answer him. They stared at their son for long minutes until, at last, his eyes flickered open.

"Mother? Father? Can I have some water?" Monica held a cup to Augustine's lips as he drank, and supported his head. His neck felt much cooler than before.

"Augustine, how do you feel?" she asked.

"I feel a little better," he replied. Then he smiled, turned over, and fell asleep. Monica slipped her arms around her husband and sobbed with relief.

"I think he's going to be alright! He's going to live, Patrick."

"Good, that's good. No need for any more tears, then," he chided her gently. They stood together for a long time, hugging and listening to their son's regular breathing, and they had forgotten all about sending for Father Crispus until there was a commotion from downstairs. Steps hurried up the stairs. Monica and Patrick slipped out into the corridor.

"Father Crispus, I'm so sorry! I thought Augustine was dying but now the fever has broken. I think he will be fine," Monica explained.

Father Crispus smiled broadly.

"That's a great relief! You don't have to apologize."

When Augustine awoke the next morning, weak but healthy, baptism was the last thing on his mind. Instead he only wanted to eat and eat and eat. Monica was just glad that her son was still alive, and Father Crispus never did write to the bishop, so the idea of Augustus' baptism was quietly forgotten.

Trail Blazers

• Augustine •
THE TRUTH SEEKER

K. C. Murdarasi

Augustine: The Truth Seeker
by K.C. Murdarasi

Although his mother was a faithful Christian, Augustine managed to stray into a sinful life. His life changed when he realized the truth of the Gospel. Augustine became a bishop and a tower of faith in the early church. His life is a glimpse into the days of Roman Africa and a powerful picture of the wisdom and durability of God's Word in a pagan culture.

ISBN: 978-1-78191-296-6

- Part of the popular Trailblazer Series
- Church father, early church history
- A tower of faith during the late days of the Roman empire.

POLYCARP
THE CROWN OF FIRE

WILLIAM CHAD NEWSOM

Polycarp: The Crown of Fire
by William Chad Newsom

Polycarp anxiously waited until the sound of marching footsteps faded away. The Praetorian guard were on the move—ready to pounce on Christians or any other 'revolutionaries' that they might find.

These were the days when the catacombs were the dark shadowy refuges of the Christians and the amphitheater was the sound of death to the believer. Polycarp, however, was one of the church leaders called on to give his life for Christ and his Kingdom... and this he counted as an honor.

To gain the Crown of Fire, he had to be willing to suffer for Christ. Did his courage hold? Or did Polycarp give in to the struggle?

Included in the book are a time line and further facts about the early church.

ISBN: 978-1-84550-041-2